Nothing

Published by August
and Northern Gallery
for Contemporary Art

ISBN: 1-902854-09-8

August
116-120 Golden Lane
London EC1Y 0TL
Tel: 020 7689 4400
dept8@augustmedia.co.uk
www.augustmedia. co.uk

Northern Gallery for
Contemporary Art
City Library & Arts Centre
Fawcett Street
Sunderland SR1 1RE

Editors: Graham Gussin,
Ele Carpenter
Project editor: Ally Ireson
Publishing director:
Nick Barley
Art director:
Stephen Coates
Design assistant:
Trude Roald
Research assistant:
Julia Schonlau

Production coordinated by:
Uwe Kraus GmbH.
Printed in Italy

This publication has
been supported by the
Arts Council of England

Publishers'
acknowledgements:
Fiona Bradley, Lise
Connellan, Simon Kennedy,
Uwe Kraus, Anne Odling-Smee, Elisabeth Scheder-Bieschin, Vanessa Smit,
Alex Stetter

The editors/curators would
like to thank all the artists
and writers who have
contributed to this book
and the exhibition, and:
Raimundas Malašauskas,
CAC, Vilnius; Charles
Esche, Rooseum, Malmö;
Jeremy Theophilus and
Aileen Daley, ACE;
Katherine Pearson, Piers
Masterson, Denise Fraser,
Debbie Fenwick, Joanna
Rowlands, Julie Crawshaw,
Dean Turnbull, Pauline
Johnson at NGCA;
Pétur Arason, Anthony
Wilkinson, Bernhard
Starkmann, Emma Smith,
Colin Fallows, Julia Langley,
Phoebe Gussin, Pierre
Bismuth, Jeremy Millar,
Chantal Crousel, Adam
Sutherland, Andrew Wilson,
Nicholas Ward-Jackson,
Anthony Reynolds, Janka
Vukmir, Paul McDonald,
David Butler, David Ward,
Bill Hall, Seth Sieglub, Mr
and Mrs Wendler, Nicholas
Logsdail, Lisa Rosendhal
at Lisson Gallery, Andrew
Renton, Florence Derieux,
Maria Lind, Robert Barry,
Waddingtons Gallery
and everyone at August

This book is published
on the occasion of the
exhibition *Nothing,*
curated by Ele Carpenter
and Graham Gussin.
A companion volume rather
than a catalogue, the book
presents texts and newly
commissioned artworks not
featured in the exhibition

Artists in the *Nothing*
exhibition:
Gaia Alessi
Francis Alÿs
Art & Language
Fiona Banner
Robert Barry
Joseph Beuys
Pierre Bismuth
James Coleman
David Connearn
Matthew Crawley
Martin Creed
Angela de la Cruz
Tacita Dean
Barry Flanagan
Ceal Floyer
Peter Fraser
Gilbert & George
Liam Gillick
Margarita Gluzberg
Kristjan Gudmundsson
Hans Haacke
Douglas Huebler
Dean Hughes
Yves Klein
Gerhard Lang
Jeremy Millar
Tatsuo Miyajima
Jonathan Monk
Gabriel Orozco
Robert Smithson
Hiroshi Sugimoto
Slaven Tolj
Keith Tyson
Lawrence Weiner
Andrew Weir
Ian Wilson
Keith Wilson
Carey Young

Touring dates:

12 April–2 June 2001
Northern Gallery for
Contemporary Art,
Sunderland

22 June–19 August 2001
Contemporary Art Centre,
Vilnius
Vokiečiu 2
2001 Vilnius
Lithuania

October–December 2001
Rooseum – Centre
for Contemporary Art
Gasverksgatan 22
Box 4097
S-20312 Malmö
Sweden

cover image:
Photograph taken
inside the CERN
particle accelerator

Funded by THE ARTS COUNCIL OF ENGLAND

City of SUNDERLAND

northern arts PROMOTING THE ARTS IN THE NORTH

NORTHERN GALLERY FOR CONTEMPORARY ART

THIS PROJECT IS BEING PART-FINANCED BY THE EUROPEAN COMMUNITY
European Regional Development Fund

Nothing

Edited by Graham Gussin and Ele Carpenter

August

Contents

I'M
COMPLETELY
EXHAUSTED

Something about Nothing
Ele Carpenter

This book emerges out of research for an exhibition of the same name, curated by myself and artist Graham Gussin. In considering content for the show, we accessed a broad range of ideas about the notion of 'nothing', which many of the exhibiting artists were referencing in their work. Having gathered such a large amount of interesting material, there was an opportunity to create something beyond the show itself which, along with visual explorations of nothing, could include perspectives from other disciplines. Sourced from cinema, philosophy and literature, these pieces of work feed into a general body of thought about absence, formlessness, invisibility and the immaterial.

To include examples of contemporary artistic practice, we invited a wider group of artists, writers and curators to make proposals for the book, asking them to acknowledge the medium of the printed page as distinct from an exhibition space. They nominated artists and suggested sources and references, as well as creating new visual and written work. The process of collecting and sifting which followed has culminated in a miscellany of ideas, one that explores the fluid territory between different disciplines and approaches – without losing a sense of the inherently complex nature of the subject. The book illustrates the fact that seemingly limitless references – value, meaning, the void, form, infinity, belief etc. – can be used to explore the idea of nothing. It also proves the difficulty of pinning down a concept which – paradoxically – is impossible to quantify. *Nothing* includes work and texts based on open-ended lines of enquiry, meanings that do not attempt definition, the exploration of non-places or imaginary space, the incidental, the pause, or the possibility of something hidden or unknown.

opposite:
I'm Completely Exhausted
Ed Ruscha
1976

As well as producing what we hope is a stimulating book, the process of creating an alternative collection of 'nothings' has in turn fed into the exhibition, offering different structures for examining the way that visual artists choose to represent the idea. Works in the show demonstrate how through an attempt to reveal either the unseen or the unknown, artists can challenge conventional notions of value by making 'something out of nothing', and 'nothing out of something'.

The *Nothing* exhibition, opening at NGCA, Sunderland, UK, continues at CAC, Vilnius, Lithuania; and then at the Rooseum, Malmö, Sweden during 2001.

Ele Carpenter
Principal Curator, Northern Gallery of Contemporary Art

opposite:
Le saut dans le vide
(Leap into the void)
Yves Klein
1960

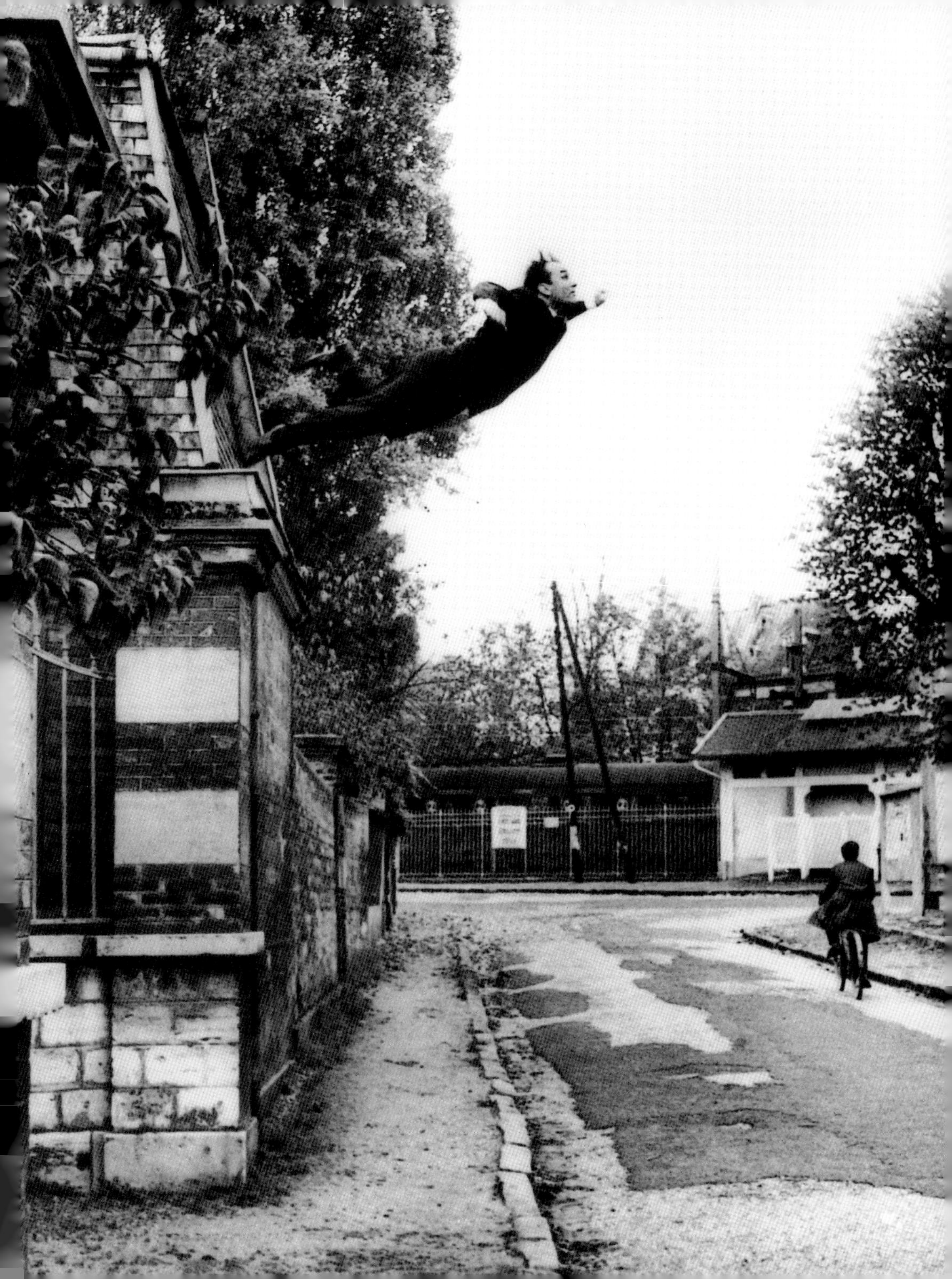

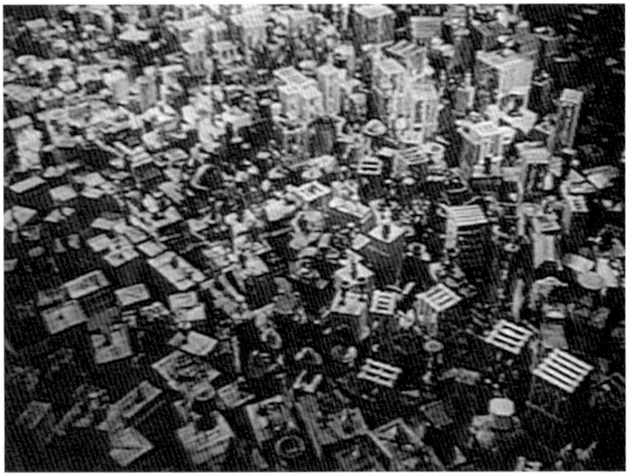

Out of It
Graham Gussin

'I don't want it to be essentially the same – I want it to be exactly the same. Because the more you look at the same thing, the more the meaning goes away, and the better and emptier you feel.'
Andy Warhol

To repeat something once is one thing, to do it over and over is another thing again. Through repetition we can be led to a place where it may be difficult to differentiate, where there may be no telling where we are. If all is the same, over and over, then nothing is distinguishable; deprived of the means to measure, of the ability to tell one moment from another, or one point from the next, we slip, merge into an enveloping sameness and lose our place. In his short story *Report on an Unknown Space Station*, J G Ballard describes an infinite architectural phenomenon which seems to swallow up time and space through endlessly repeating the same symmetrical elements; and the work of Jorge Luis Borges often touches on the idea of a labyrinth as a straight line, invisible and unceasing.

So endless repetition can take us nowhere, to a non-state, a kind of Utopia – meaning literally 'no-place' – or perhaps towards what philosopher Gregory Bateson terms a 'plateau': a 'continuous, self-vibrating region of intensities whose development avoids any orientation toward a culminating point or external end.' Actions like ritualistic shaking or repeating a specific sound in the form of a mantra or chant are known ways of approaching or achieving altered states, of releasing individuals into an ego-less, trance-like zone in which there is no sense of time and where sense of self is so diffused that it ceases to be self and becomes all. Through such profound integration, differentiation (its inverse) becomes impossible; this is repetition registered as a kind of vibration.

opposite:
Citizen Kane (still)
director Orson Welles
1941

So in the right conditions, time and space are superseded so that one may possibly reach Nirvana, a release attained by the extinction of all desires and individual existence; it is interesting to note that the literal translation from the Sanskrit of 'nirvana' is 'a blowing out'.

In Stanley Kubrick's film *The Shining* (1980), Jack Nicholson's character types the same sentence over and over again as he sinks into madness. Instead of release, he finds himself imprisoned, spiralling inwards towards a point of terrible destructiveness. The action of repeatedly typing the same group of words represents a kind of ritual, mesmerising and numbing; we can imagine it being done first without needing to look, then without feeling the keys, then without even thinking... The way in which the resulting text appears as an image demonstrates that there is also a powerful potential for disorientation or voiding in the application of repetition to representation, as well as to action. Laid out in an unceasing line, the amassed words of each identical ten-word sentence form a cloud of activity, one which seems impossible to follow; as we look at the page, like Nicholson's madman, we rapidly become blinded and lost. Clearly there is nowhere to go from here, every step is the same, on and on into oblivion...

Similarly, the image of Christ in Andy Warhol's *Christ 112 Times* empties itself before our eyes, becoming void through the artist forcing it to surrender its uniqueness. We could also consider that a single image or object, or particularly a person, can be seen so many times that they become overexposed, as if repeated showing (without the correct precautions being taken) must lead to invisibility and emptiness – exposure can ultimately cause stars to collapse in on themselves. This notion of disappearance through appearance is particular to the age of mechanical reproduction, intimately linked with photography and its literal potential for overexposure, where subjects may be 'lost' through too much light being received by the camera. This notion of showing, overload and disintegration is related to accumulation, in itself a kind of repetition. Through acquiring possessions to an extreme degree, we may in fact become dispossessed, as shown by the view of Citizen Kane's collection of artefacts (from jigsaws to 'dames without heads') in the closing sequence of Orson Welles's film. This is a demonstration of accumulation taken to the point of overload, where a wealth of

All work and no play makes Jack a dull boy. All work and no play makes objects or figures reaches critical mass and becomes a collective nothing.

'Sensory Deprivation Tanks' were developed in the 1960s in order to explore the mind's relationship to the body. Cocooned in one of these facilities, the user is able to artificially experience total isolation, and lose all sense of their physical boundaries (no beginning and no end – Bateson's plateau again). The development of SDTs (renamed for commercial purposes as 'floatation tanks'), and their appearance on the market tracks our desire to acquire nothingness, a state of absorption where there is no information to process. The tanks offer us a powerful confrontation with absence. Ken Russell's *Altered States* (1980) begins with this state as its subject, taking the anxiety it can provoke to dramatic extremes. Following immersion in a sensory deprivation tank, the film's central character becomes totally divorced from the knowledge and sense of identity they had previously held. When the tank finally opens, a primitive being emerges; it is as if the character's mind has had to retreat back into itself in order to refute an existential vacuum.

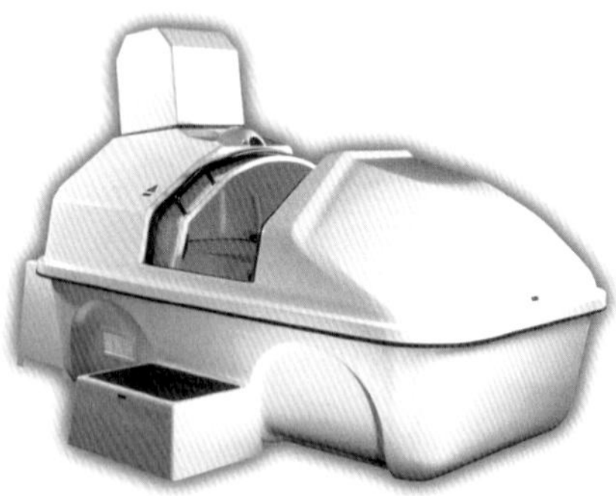

Floatation tank (model: Apollo ELV)

The idea of being taken is perhaps useful to us in thinking about disappearance, the act of being pulled in or enveloped by a force. Here, with the force of gravity, magnetism or fascination acting upon us, we are drawn towards an active force rather than being propelled away from one. It appears that as well as being sucked into an abyss we can also surrender ourselves to one willingly; depending on perspective, a vacuum can either be a trap or a desired abstraction. George Sluizer's film *The Vanishing* (1988) deals brilliantly with this dichotomy, presenting us with the notion of a trap that is also the only way out, here characterised by the ultimate terror – the state of being buried alive. Compelled by uncertainty and the unknown details of his lover's disappearance, the film's central character is lured into a subterranean prison; a place that offers him final release from obsession through understanding his lover's fate – his death repeats hers. In Sluizer's words, he was '...attempting to find the point where the one thing changes to something else'.

Both a fear of and a human need for the formless, for something dimly remembered yet absolutely necessary, are indicated through all of this. Being 'blank' or 'vacant' ('preoccupied' is a term often used to describe this state, which is strange when what we are attempting to describe is emptiness) is a productive space, the desire to disengage and close down being like a reflex, a simple consequence, an adjustment.

> Heaven
> Heaven is a place
> A place where nothing
> Nothing ever happens
> *Heaven*, Talking Heads, 1979

The Vanishing (still)
director George Sluizer
1988

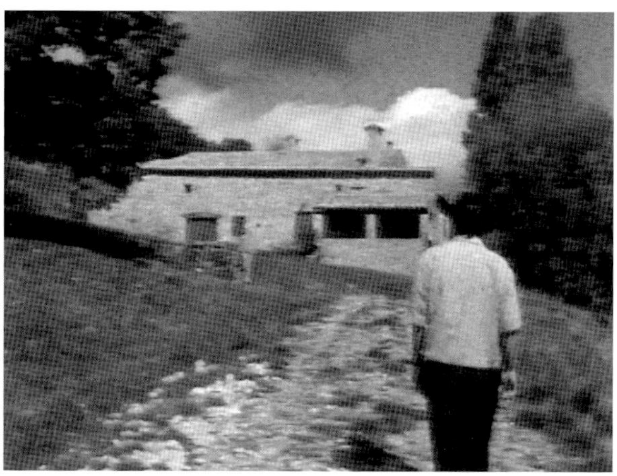

From Zero to Nothing in No Time
Francis McKee

1.

Nothing is impossible. Or, put another way, 'nothing' is a concept so fraught with paradox and contradictions that it defeats definition. The flipside of nothing is something and each attempt to consider the idea of nothing reveals yet another 'thing' or entity – no matter how mundane, microscopic or previously imperceptible. In such circumstances, it becomes more useful to discuss the importance of the concept to human culture and the various guises in which it has appeared through history.

In his 'Essay on Nothing' (1949), John Cage claimed that 'Nothing more than nothing can be said'. He had, of course, famously begun that lecture by stating 'I have nothing to say and I am saying it'. Despite the apparent pitfalls of attempting to articulate any thought on this particular subject, there is now a foolish and brave pantheon of writers, philosophers and scientists who have dedicated themselves to the elaboration of the subject.

While each of them has had to struggle with the linguistic challenge of 'saying nothing', linguists themselves have noticed that this is effectively what we do most of the time. In 1923, Bronislav Malinowski identified two main elements in conversation – the informational and the *phatic* (from the Greek word for 'to speak') – and he described the latter saying:

> Phatic communion... is a type of speech in which ties of union are created by a mere exchange of words... Words in phatic communion... fulfil a social function and that is their principal aim... Phatic communication is used to establish social relationships rather than impart information.[1]

Published in the same year that James Joyce began his 'Work in Progress' (later to become *Finnegans Wake*) and a year before André

Breton's surrealist manifesto, Malinowski had stumbled on the notion that we are all talking about nothing most of the time, and that this is something to cherish.

2.

'For to know nothing is nothing, not to want to know anything likewise, but to be beyond knowing anything, to know you are beyond knowing anything, that is when peace enters in, to the soul of the incurious seeker.'
Samuel Beckett, *Molloy*[2]

3.

The phatic element of John Cage's writing is the true vehicle for his thoughts. Discussing his 'Essay on Nothing', the dance critic Jill Johnston noted that:

> There is no logic in Cage's lectures (unless it be the logic of style, which is everywhere in evidence); he merely describes situations, or gives spontaneous voice to convictions and insights, or rambles coherently about nothing.[3]

As if to undermine even the faintest possibility that his texts might still be restored to order by the conventional reading habits of his audience, Cage supplements his book *Silence* with various deliberately aimless anecdotes, as in the following examples:

> Once I was visiting my Aunt Marge. She was doing her laundry. She turned to me and said, 'You know? I love this machine much more than I do your Uncle Walter.'

and

> When Vera Williams first noticed that I was interested in wild mushrooms, she told her children not to touch any of them because they were all deadly poisonous. A few days later she bought a steak at Martino's and decided to serve it smothered with mushrooms. When she started to cook the mushrooms, the children all stopped whatever they were doing and watched her attentively. When she served dinner, they all burst into tears.

These stories, scattered throughout his lectures, echo the structure of the Zen *koan* – a short, enigmatic text given to a monk's pupil as a puzzle which may lead to enlightenment. Certainly, Cage was influenced by the ethos of Zen and the work of Alan Watts, the central figure in Zen's transmission to the West. Cage is always careful, however, to undermine any sense of gaining 'something' through enlightenment, and tellingly included a Japanese monk's lament – 'Now that I'm enlightened, I'm just as miserable as ever'.[4]

4.

'It's something that Impressionist painters used to do. Whenever they were unsure of the true colour of something, they'd look at its reflection in a piece of black glass. They thought that the only way they could ever see the true nature of something was to reflect it onto something dark.'
Douglas Coupland, *Miss Wyoming*[5]

5.

In January 1979, Andy Warhol exhibited his 'shadow' paintings – a large sequence of abstract canvases which he described as 'one painting... with parts'. The origin of the images on which they are based remains uncertain. His studio assistant, Ronnie Cutrone, believes they were taken from a series of photographs of abstract maquettes in the Factory. Warhol himself said that they had their origin in 'a photo of a shadow in my studio'. Lynne Cooke, in an essay on the paintings, notes alternative histories which claim respectively that they were based on: photographs of children's building blocks; the shape cast by an erect penis; shadows cast by the Empire State Building.[6]

Each canvas was restricted to a single colour and the imagery dominated by two abstract compositions, with large, sweeping brushstrokes visible in many of the pictures. The paintings were hung low, edge to edge, in a continuous frieze around the gallery with no deliberate sequencing. Julian Schnabel, describing *Shadows* for a 1989 catalogue remarked that 'There is almost nothing on them. Yet they seem to be pictures of something.'

It is tempting to pursue the circularity of Schnabel's statement and conclude that the 'something' he detects in the paintings is 'nothing' and the 'nothing' which Warhol confronts in *Shadows* works on many levels. Victor Stoichita, in *A Short History of the Shadow*, traces the impulse for the series of images back to a photograph of Andy Warhol and Giorgio de Chirico taken sometime in 1974. Both

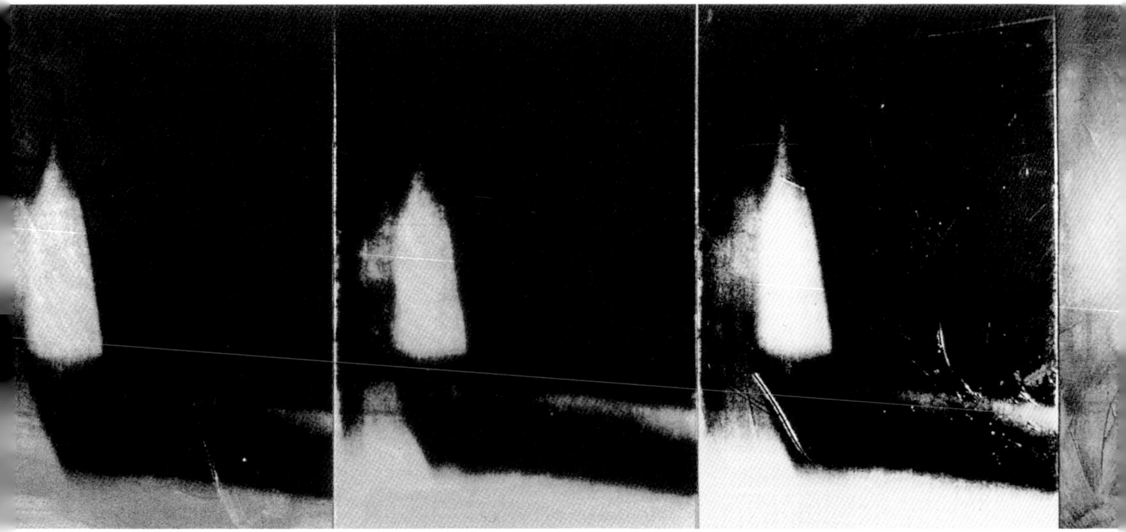

Shadows
Andy Warhol
1979

artists stand in deep shadow – de Chirico stares balefully at the camera like an old master of horror, while Warhol seems to wince as if suddenly possessed by a dark force. Four years later, in November 1978, de Chirico died. One month later, Warhol began the series of paintings which became *Shadows*.

For Stoichita, the work 'unveils Warhol's debt to de Chirico' as he 'replaces the Italian master's shadow stories with storyless shadows.' For Victor Bockris, Warhol's biographer, the context of his subject's life is just as important at this point as any homage to a dying master. Chronicling the Factory scene at this time he writes:

> The façade of good times was cracking. The nonstop night-time revelry began to take a toll... All the major players in Andy's life except Vincent Fremont suffered from drug and liquor problems and started breaking down around him.[7]

Shadows, despite its abstraction, documents this entropy. His sequence of silkscreened photographs are fractured glances into the margins of his life, echoed in the self-portraits of the same period where he plays with negative images or is haunted by his own shadow on the Factory walls.

6.

'Movement

The feeling of a ship or a train or a bus beneath me, each with its different rituals, its different rhythms. A destination was useful because it was a substitute for purpose; it answered any question I was likely to be asked. Movement became my reason for being, my excuse. Movement for its own sake. I forget who it was who wrote about the importance of doing nothing, how the art of doing nothing is one that most people seem to have forgotten. Well, I decided to resurrect the art. In doing nothing, I would be reduced to what I was moving through. I would, quite literally, become part of the scenery. I would blend, immerse. Dissolve.

And wasn't this, also, in the end, a way of dealing with death? Death, which is the root of all anxiety. Death, which requires us to justify ourselves. Death, which makes us believe in God.

All that I could happily dispense with.

Do nothing. Whatever happens, happens. Let it come.'

Rupert Thomson, *The Book of Revelation*[8]

7.

There are now several histories of zero and the concept of nothing on the market. Like many popular science books they start easily and gradually work towards the mathematics of the phenomenon. It is at this point that much of the general population find themselves floundering. Very possibly the mathematics of nothing is intensely moving, and for scientists the real excitement of mathematics lies in its abstraction from the world around us. For example, John D Barrow, in *The Book of Nothing*, writes:

> In the end mathematics was too great an empire to remain intimately linked to physical reality. At first, mathematicians took their ideas of counting and geometry largely from the world around them. They believed there to be a single geometry and a single logic. In the nineteenth century they began to see further. These simple systems of mathematics they had abstracted from the natural world provided models from which new abstract structures, defined solely by the rules for combining their symbols, could be created. Mathematics was potentially infinite.[9]

This is essentially where the real story of the vacuum universe takes off, but it is also the moment at which something more intimate vanishes. Zero, nothing and the cipher have a humbler life among the general population where they remain tied to the physical world, denoting the accidents, breaks and interstices along the course from birth to death.

In an interview later entitled 'On Philosophy', Gilles Deleuze calibrates theory to a more humanistic pitch when he talks of the empty spaces in his own curriculum vitae:

> If you want to apply bio-bibliographical criteria to me, I confess I wrote my first book fairly early on, and then produced nothing more for eight years. I know what I was doing, where and how I lived during those years, but I know it only abstractly, rather as if someone else was relating memories that I believe but don't really have. It's like a hole in my life, an eight-year hole. That's what I find interesting in people's lives, the holes, the gaps, sometimes dramatic, but sometimes not dramatic at all. There are catalepsies, or a kind of sleep-walking through a number of years, in most lives. Maybe it's in these holes that movement takes place.[10]

In the public arena, as celebrity and the search for biographical detail reaches new levels of intensity, these gaps in peoples lives are assuming new importance. With figures as diverse as Arthur Rimbaud, Greta Garbo and Howard Hughes it is the unknown and apparently empty years they spent away from the spotlight that now assume almost mythic status.

Even among these names, the writer Thomas Pynchon looms larger than most. His twenty-year disappearance from public view and from publishing left a void that could only be filled by increasingly bizarre rumours and legend. Even before he vanished it was notable how invisible he had become with few photos in circulation and few biographical facts available to the media. By the late 1980s, while fans were speculating that he may be writing under the guise of 'Wanda Tinasky' – a homeless woman in California – several hazy photographs of the author briefly surfaced. To the shock of the media and the public, it was clear that Pynchon had a perfectly respectable address in the Upper West Side of New York where he was raising a family and living an unspectacular life.

Around this time, Pynchon began to publish again – first with a preface to a collection of his older short stories, entitled *Slow Learner,* and later with two novels, *Vineland* and *Mason & Dixon*. In *Slow Learner*, echoing Deleuze, Pynchon views his earlier self as if looking at a stranger:

> My first reaction, rereading these stories, was oh my God, accompanied by physical symptoms we shouldn't dwell upon. My second thought was about some kind of a wall-to-wall rewrite. These two impulses have given way to one of those episodes of middle-aged tranquility, in which I now pretend to have reached a level of clarity about the young writer I was back then. I mean I can't very well just 86 this guy from my life. On the other hand, if through some as yet undeveloped technology I were to run into him today, how comfortable would I feel about lending him money, or for that matter even stepping down the street to have a beer and talk over old times?[11]

What Thomas Pynchon the Elder has learnt slowly during his long 'catalepsy' is the impressive extent of his own ignorance, the geography and the local economy of the empty spaces that are in all our lives:

> The trouble with many of us is that at the earlier stages of life we think we know everything – or to put it more usefully, we are often unaware of the scope and structure of our ignorance. Ignorance is not just a blank space

> on a person's mental map. It has contours and coherence, and for all I know rules of operation as well.[12]

To inhabit such territory demands a strategy for survival – an expertise in doing nothing. Obligingly, in 1993, Pynchon published an essay in the *New York Times Book Review* on the subject of 'Sloth', detailing the history of this sin. Arguing that it is 'the vernacular of everyday moral life', he outlines the ways in which we do nothing or do something at such an imperceptible pace that we appear to do nothing and thereby evade attention and the chore of making difficult choices:

> Though it has never lost its deepest notes of mortal anxiety, it never gets as painful as outright despair, or as real, for it is despair bought at a discount price, a deliberate turning against faith in anything because of the inconvenience faith presents to the pursuit of quotidian lusts, angers and the rest. The compulsive pessimist's last defense – stay still enough and the blade of the scythe, somehow, will pass by – Sloth is our background radiation, our easy-listening station – it is everywhere, and no longer noticed.[13]

When another author, David Bowman, investigated the invisibility of Thomas Pynchon he discovered that his whereabouts were in fact well known and that not only had one previous researcher given up because it was too easy but that CNN had tracked him down and captured him on film in one afternoon. Despite this, Pynchon remains badly documented and, even in the pirate archives of the internet, photos of the writer are scarce. Clearly we need his anonymity as much as he does and we are conspiring to maintain it. For Bowman, who eventually viewed the CNN tape, something was lost: 'I'm still left a little sad. For me, the twentieth century is over early – the last free man has been hunted and trussed.'[14]

8.

'I remember now that Feldman spoke of shadows. He said that the sounds were not sounds but shadows. They are obviously sounds; that's why they are shadows. Every something is an echo of nothing.'
John Cage, 'Lecture on Something'[15]

> From ancient China there is a description of a vibrato technique: Remarkable is the ting-yin, where the vacillating movement of the finger should be so subtle as to be hardly noticeable. Some handbooks say that

> one should not move the finger at all, but let the timbre be influenced by the pulsation of the blood in the fingertips pressing the string down on the board a little more heavily than usual.
>
> Such extreme sensitivity of touch is of the essence in a performance of Feldman's music. In the piano pieces the depressed key is gently eased back to position to minimise the obtrusive sound of the key mechanism, time is allowed for the minutest of harmonics to resound, and at the end of the phrases fingers steal away from the keys noiselessly.
> John Tilbury, 'On Playing Feldman'[16]

> Morton Feldman has written an opera in one act to an original text by Samuel Beckett. Entitled *Neither* it is scored for soprano solo and full orchestra, and was commissioned by Rome Opera, where it receives its first performance on May 13, 1977, conducted by Marcello Panni...
>
> When the text eventually arrived, Feldman was struck by the space between sentences – a form of visual punctuation. His natural, if idiosyncratic, response was to concentrate on each line in isolation.'First of all, like a conventional composer, I started to scan the first sentence: To and fro in shadow from inner to outer shadow...'
> Howard Skempton, 'Beckett as Librettist'[17]

10.

Often nothing is no more than something imperceptible to our senses or beyond the reach of our technologies. Black holes – a modern emblem of nothingness – are the clearest example of this. The gravity at work in a collapsing star is so powerful light cannot escape its pull and so we cannot see it as a phenomenon. Yet, through physics and mathematics, scientists have been able to confirm their existence. In a simple primer on black holes Kitty Ferguson offers an explanation of what happens:

> Gravity was the force that gave birth to the star in a cloud of gas. It was the force that kept the star in balance for all those years, not allowing it to fly apart but also contributing to the processes that prevented its collapse. Now, after millions or even billions of years have passed, gravity is the force that claims the star as its victim, squeezing all its enormous mass to something the size of the sun... then to the size of the earth... to the size of the moon... to the size of London... St James's Park... the lake in the park... a duck on the lake... a tennis ball... a marble... the head of a pin... the point of a pin... a microbe... For a star ending up more massive than about 3 solar masses, we know of no power capable of halting this

> catastrophic collapse. The star continues to crunch down even after it has become a black hole. It's best to think of a black hole not as a star, but as what happens to spacetime around a star that goes on collapsing to near infinite density.[18]

Beyond this point, the understanding of the phenomenon involves gravitational redshift, quantum vacuums, virtual particles, antiparticles, and the Einstein-Rosen Bridge or 'wormholes'. It is here that most of us turn to *Star Trek* for further elucidation, finding the science more imposing and less exciting than the metaphor and the potential narratives it might generate. For the moment it is the capability of black holes and wormholes to transform the landscape of our imagination which has the greater resonance.

In art too, the imperceptible has the same ability to capture human imagination. In the late 1960s, the artist Robert Barry used this fact as the basis for a series of works focusing his audience on potentially infinite concepts while demonstrating the finite boundaries of human and technological perception. In his 'Inert Gas' pieces, Barry would release commercially bottled 'noble gases' back into the earth's atmosphere and in his 'Carrier Waves' works, he had small transmitters constructed which would blot out all radio waves within the immediate vicinity of the gallery. The latter pieces in particular were seen as sculptural by the artist who has since described that, saying:

> Sculpture is the only word I could think of for it, because they were, the boundaries were, theoretically, infinite. But because our technology isn't infinite, there were limits as to where we could actually perceive this piece to be. And so technically, there were bounds; conceptually, it was infinite.[19]

In another context, he defends the infinitesimal nature of these works in the following way:

> These forms certainly do exist, they are controlled and have their own characteristics. They are made of various kinds of energy which exist outside the narrow arbitrary limits of our own senses. I use various devices to produce the energy, detect it, measure it, and define its form.
>
> By just being in this show, I'm making known the existence of the work... there are many other possibilities which I intend to explore – and I'm sure there are a lot of things we don't yet know about which exist

> in the space around us, and although we don't see them or feel them, we somehow know they are out there.[20]

Barry made this work in the vanguard of the conceptual movement which emerged at the end of the 1960s but it is clear that interest in the possibility of depicting absence was not confined only to that group of artists. While Warhol investigated shadows throughout the 1970s, others such as Gerhard Richter explored ideas of nothing through painting in the mid-1980s. Richter's 'Grey' paintings in particular gave him a vehicle for his own definition of the subject:

> Grey. It makes no statement whatever; it evokes neither feelings not associations; it is really neither visible or invisible. Its inconspicuousness gives it the capacity to mediate, to make visible, in a positively illusionistic way, like a photograph. It has the capacity that no other colour has, to make 'nothing' visible.
>
> To me, grey, is the welcome and only possible equivalent for indifference, noncommitment, absence of opinion, absence of shape. But grey, like formlessness and the rest, can be real only as an idea, and so all I can do is create a colour nuance that means grey but is not it. The painting is then a mixture of grey as a fiction and grey as a visible designated area of colour.[21]

In a series of 'Notes' from this period there is a clear urgency in Richter's confrontation with 'the monstrousness of the Void' and he remarks at one point that his work on his abstract paintings is the 'only natural thing', adding 'I know nothing, I can do nothing, I understand nothing, I know nothing. Nothing'. At other times, he echoes Robert Barry in his awareness of the limits of our senses, science and philosophy:

> It is not possible to visualize Nothing. One way to gain some idea of that terrible state is through the impossibility of visualising anything before, after or alongside the universe. Now since we very much want this visualisation, but know it only as one that we can never have, it is an impossibility that we experience, existentially, as an absolute limit.[22]

For Richter, as for Robert Barry and the scientists attempting to define black holes, there are a set of physical limitations which eventually shade into philosophical paradox as they wrestle with the impossibility of making absence present.

In *Underworld* (1999), Don DeLillo uncovers another set of

limitations that come into play when we are confronted with an embodiment of Nothing in everyday life. One of the novel's characters, Brian Glassic, drives out to a landfill site on Staten Island and surveys the enormous operation in progress to deal with garbage:

> He imagined he was watching the construction of the Great Pyramid at Giza – only this was twenty-five times bigger... All this ingenuity and labor, this delicate effort to fit maximum waste into diminishing space... And the thing was organic, ever growing and shifting, its shape computer-plotted by the day and the hour...
>
> The mountain was here, unconcealed, but no one saw it or thought about it, no one knew it existed except the engineers and teamsters and local residents, a unique cultural deposit, fifty million tons by the time they top it off, carved and modeled, and no talked about it but the men and women who tried to manage it...[23]

Just as weeds are the dark reflection of plants, so rubbish is the state of nothing into which derelict objects are banished. In this case, however, the mountain of 'nothing' is imperceptible because we choose not to see it. As DeLillo's character notes, while contemplating 'all that soaring garbage': 'The biggest secrets are the ones spread open before us.'

11.

'For although in a certain sense and for light-minded persons non-existent things can be more easily and irresponsibly presented in words than existing things, for the serious and conscientious historian it is just the reverse. Nothing is harder, yet nothing is more necessary, than to speak of certain things whose existence is neither demonstrable nor probable. The very fact that serious and conscientious men treat them as existing things brings them a step closer to existence and to the possibility of being born.'
Hermann Hesse, *The Glass Bead Game*[24]

12.

Thursday night, 31 July 1930. At 9.40 p.m. on CBS Radio, James La Curto portrayed 'The Shadow' for the first time in *The Detective Story Hour*. The show ran from 1930 to 1954, and after The Shadow began to appear as a character not just a narrator, the part was played for a year by Orson Welles in 1938. Victor

Bockris records that, as a child, Andy Warhol was an avid listener to the programme:

> Hitler's speeches, Churchill's impassioned and defiant voice and Edward R Murrow's broadcasts from London brought the sounds of the war into the Warholas' living room. According to Mina Serbin, all Andy ever talked about was how many people were dying. His favourite radio character was The Shadow, whose signature statement was, 'Who knows what evil lurks in the hearts of men? The Shadow knows...'[25]

Andy knew too. By 1978, beginning his *Shadows* series, he knew that the Factory, like a black hole, was exerting a fatal gravitational pull. Anyone in its orbit was collapsing under the strain. He himself was a slowly dying star, camouflaging the seriousness of his work under a layer of dismissive comments (*Shadows* was just 'disco décor' he remarked in a *New York Magazine* article on the exhibition).

14.
'We start, then, with nothing, pure zero. But this is not the nothing of negation. For not means other than, and other is merely a synonym of the ordinal numeral second. As such it implies a first; while the present pure zero is prior to every first. The nothing of negation is the nothing of death, which comes second to, or after, everything. But this pure zero is the nothing of not having been born. There is no individual thing, no compulsion, outward nor inward, no law. It is the germinal nothing, in which the whole universe is involved or foreshadowed. As such, it is absolutely undefined and unlimited possibility – boundless possibility. There is no compulsion and no law. It is boundless freedom.'
Charles S Peirce, *Logic of Events*[26]

15.
September 1977. Andy Warhol lent over seventy objects to the New York Museum of American Folk Art for an exhibition curated by his friend, Sandra Brant. Amid the surrealistic bric-a-bric and primitive examples of early US product design lay Warhol's favourite piece – an eighteenth-century pale blue door and doorframe. 'I like the door best,' he said. 'You can go in and out of it and still go nowhere.'[27]

see page 199 for footnotes

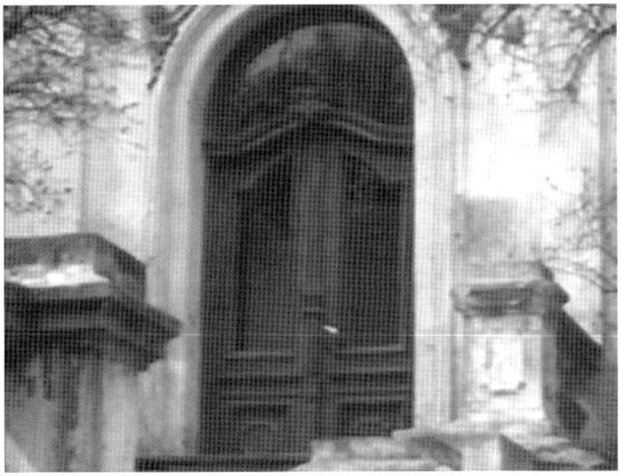

The Invisible Man (still)
USSR, 1984

WIPED OFF THE FACE OF THE EARTH

previous spread:
Wiped Off The Face Of The Earth
Lawrence Weiner
1998

below:
Condensation Cube
Hans Haacke
1965

opposite:
Der Wanderer über dem Nebelmeer
(Wanderer above the sea of fog)
Caspar David Friedrich
1818

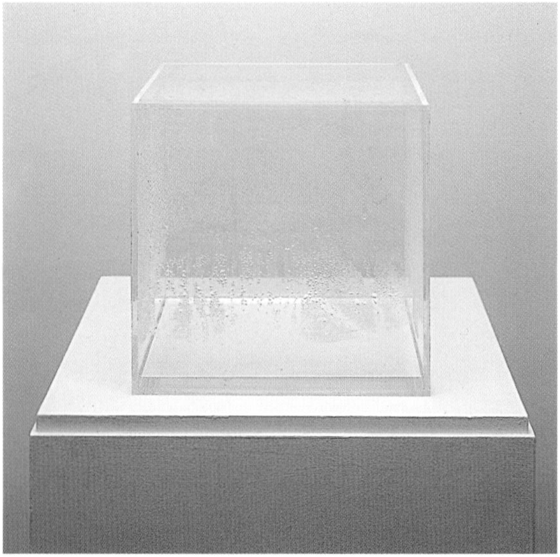

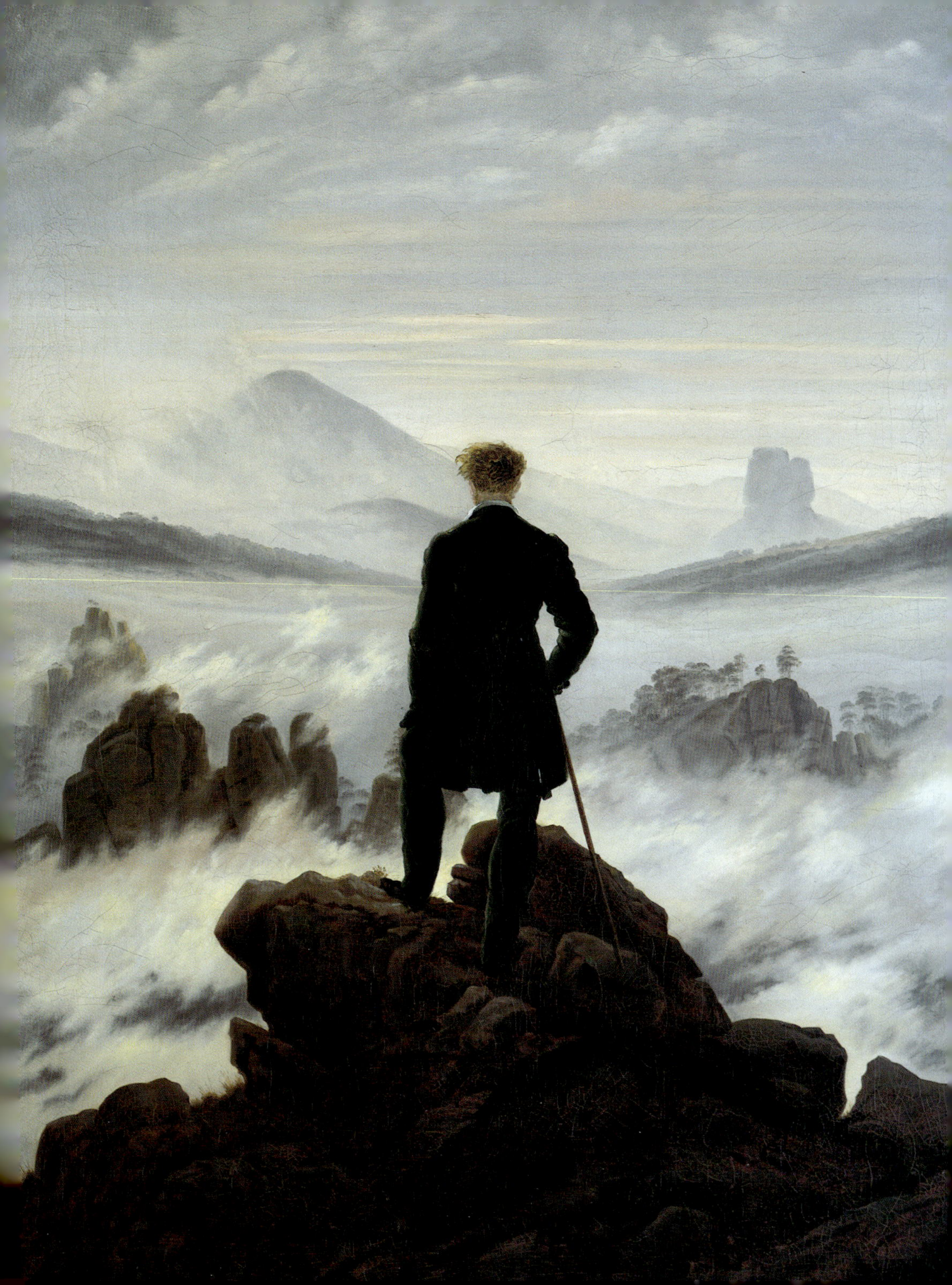

below:
Whirlpool (Eye of the Storm)
Dennis Oppenheim
1973

opposite:
Proposal for Vacuum
Jeremy Millar
1998

overleaf:
Artist in a Disappearing Landscape
Alexander and Susan Maris
1999

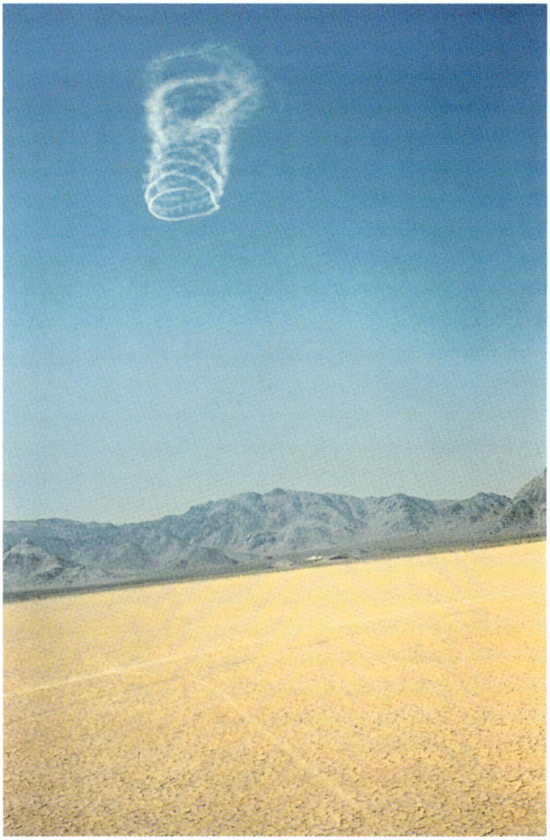

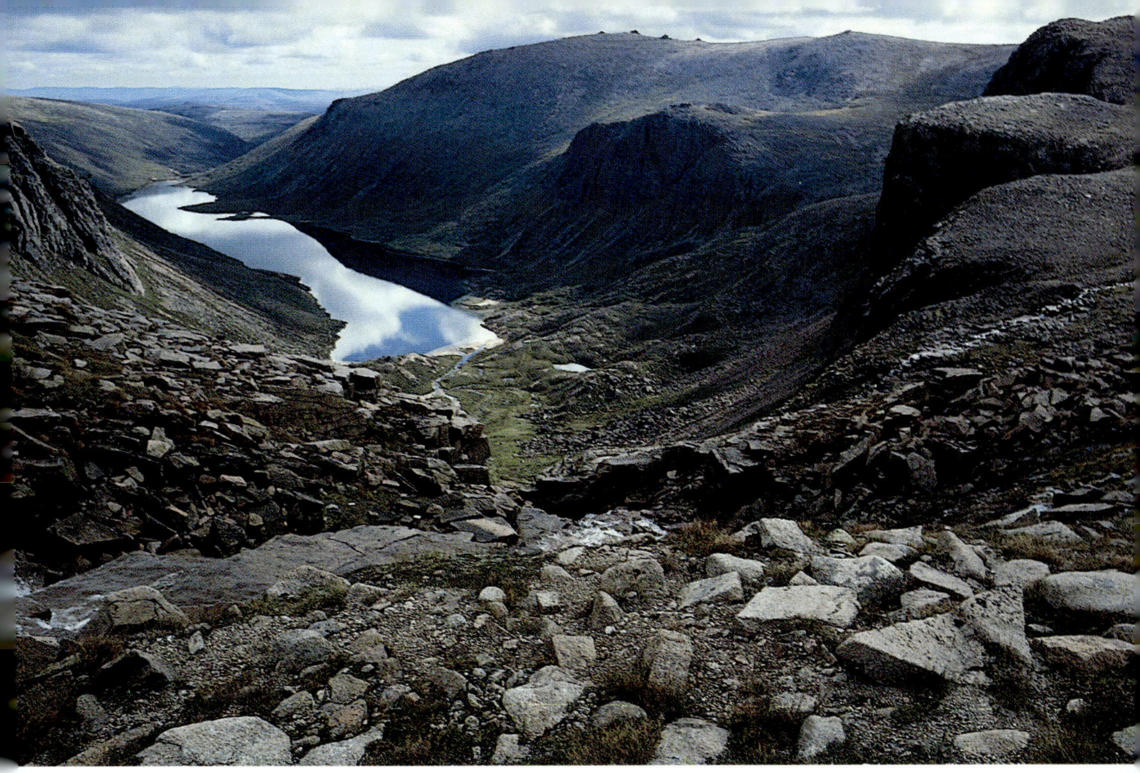

A large hollow glass sphere is placed on a hillside in northern Scotland. The air is removed from the sphere leaving a vacuum; the sphere contains nothing.

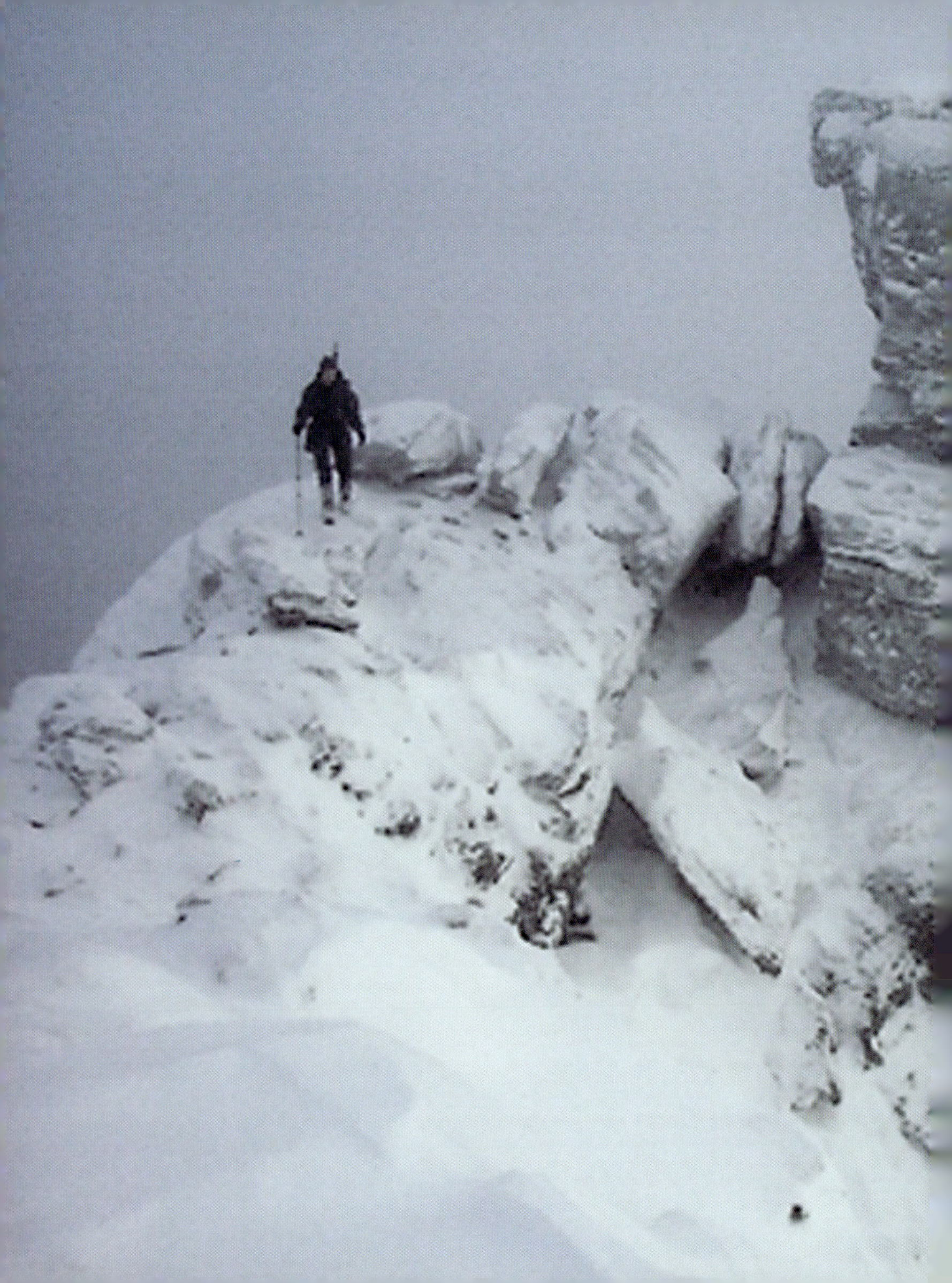

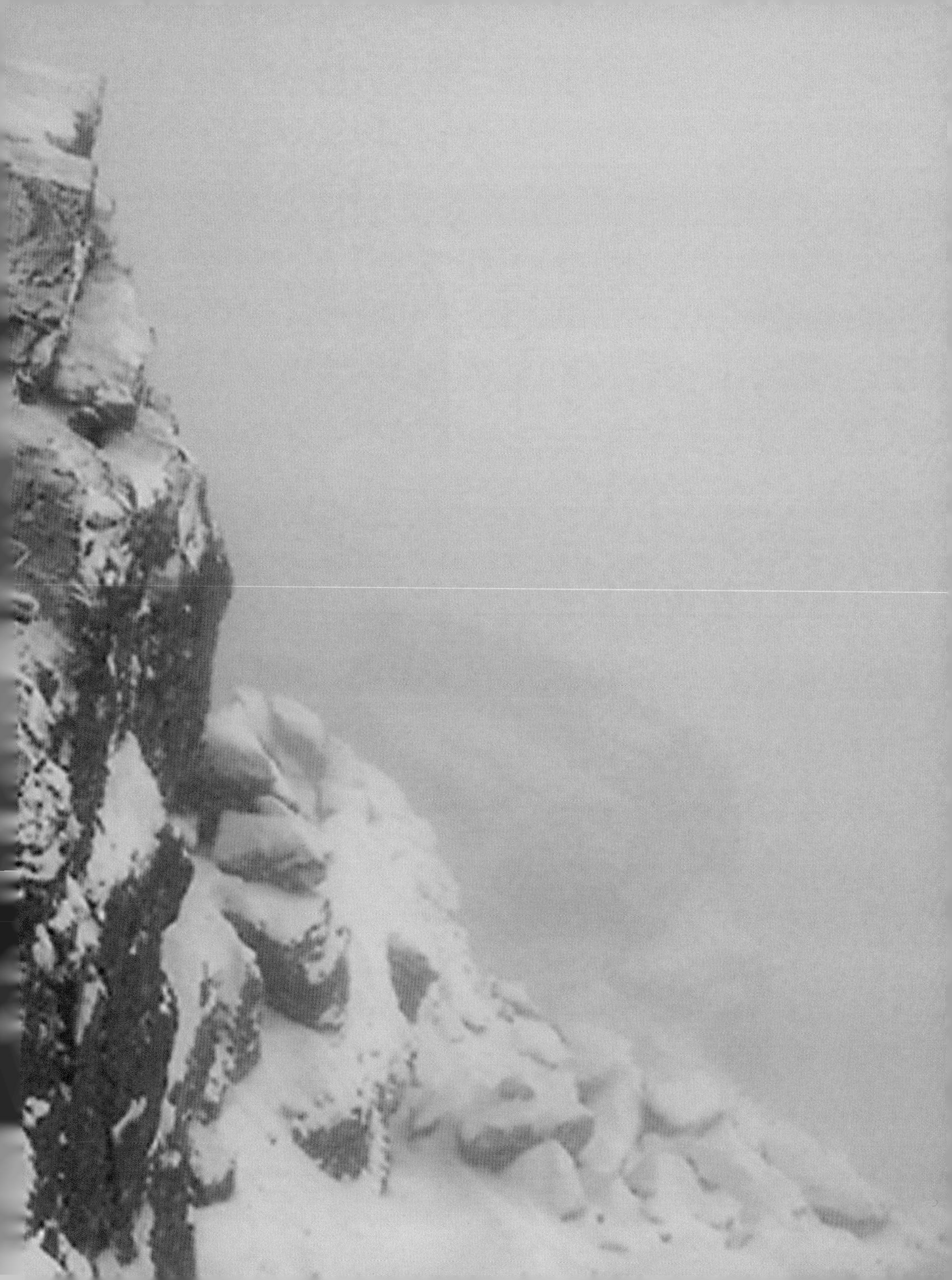

The Hunting of the Snark (map)
Lewis Carroll
1876

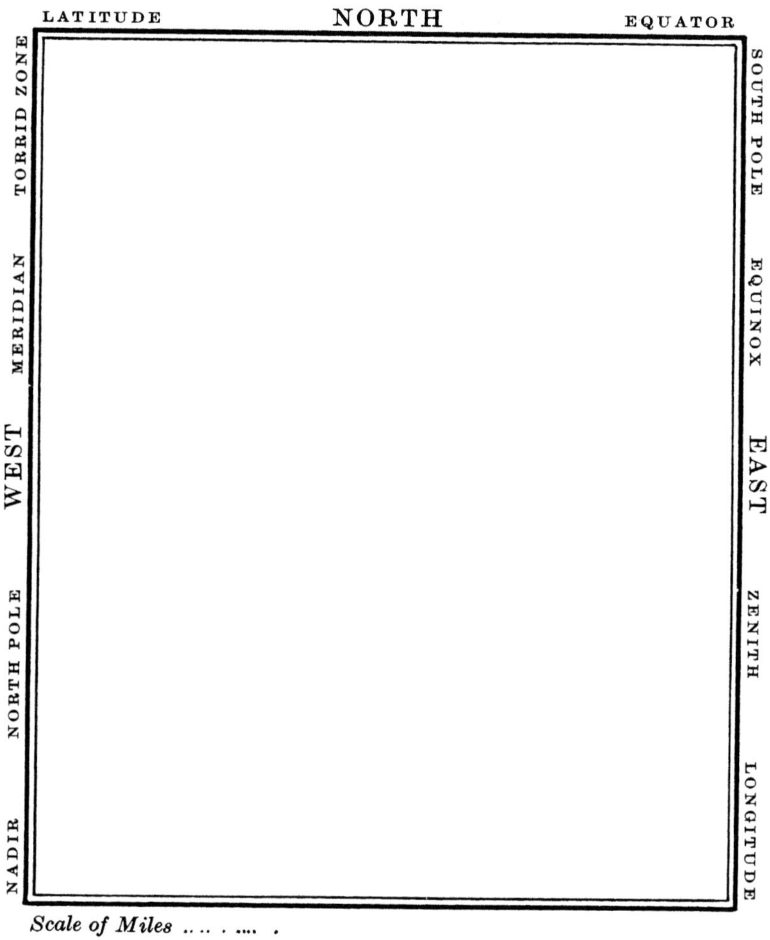

Scott of the Antarctic and 'The Last Great Wilderness'

Captain Robert Falcon Scott first sailed to the Antarctic in 1901 on the Royal Research Ship *Discovery*, his drive to 'conquer' the South Pole eventually leading to the infamous, fatal expedition of 1910–1912.

Scott and his companions did reach the Pole, but only hours after it had already been 'claimed' by the Norwegian, Roald Amundsen; Scott and his party subsequently perished in severe conditions before they were able to return to base. In his journal for the day they reached the Pole, only to realise they were not the first, Scott wrote: 'Great God! This is an awful place and terrible enough for us to have laboured to it without the reward of priority (17th January 1911).'

The principal success of Scott's first expedition in 1901 had been to reach a record-breaking southern latitude, going beyond the 80° South previously attained by other groups. As Scott and his party reached the limit of the territory mapped by former expeditions, the charts that had guided them ran out into blank white paper.

We can only wonder at the sheer impact of experiencing that point of coincidence between chart and wilderness on both the bodies and minds of men so steeped in the importance of objective knowledge. The empty chart seems an apt metaphor for what actually appeared before them: an expanse of white space stretching as far as the eye could see – perhaps the best possible map of 'the last great wilderness' that was Antarctica.

Katrina Brown and Nathan Coley

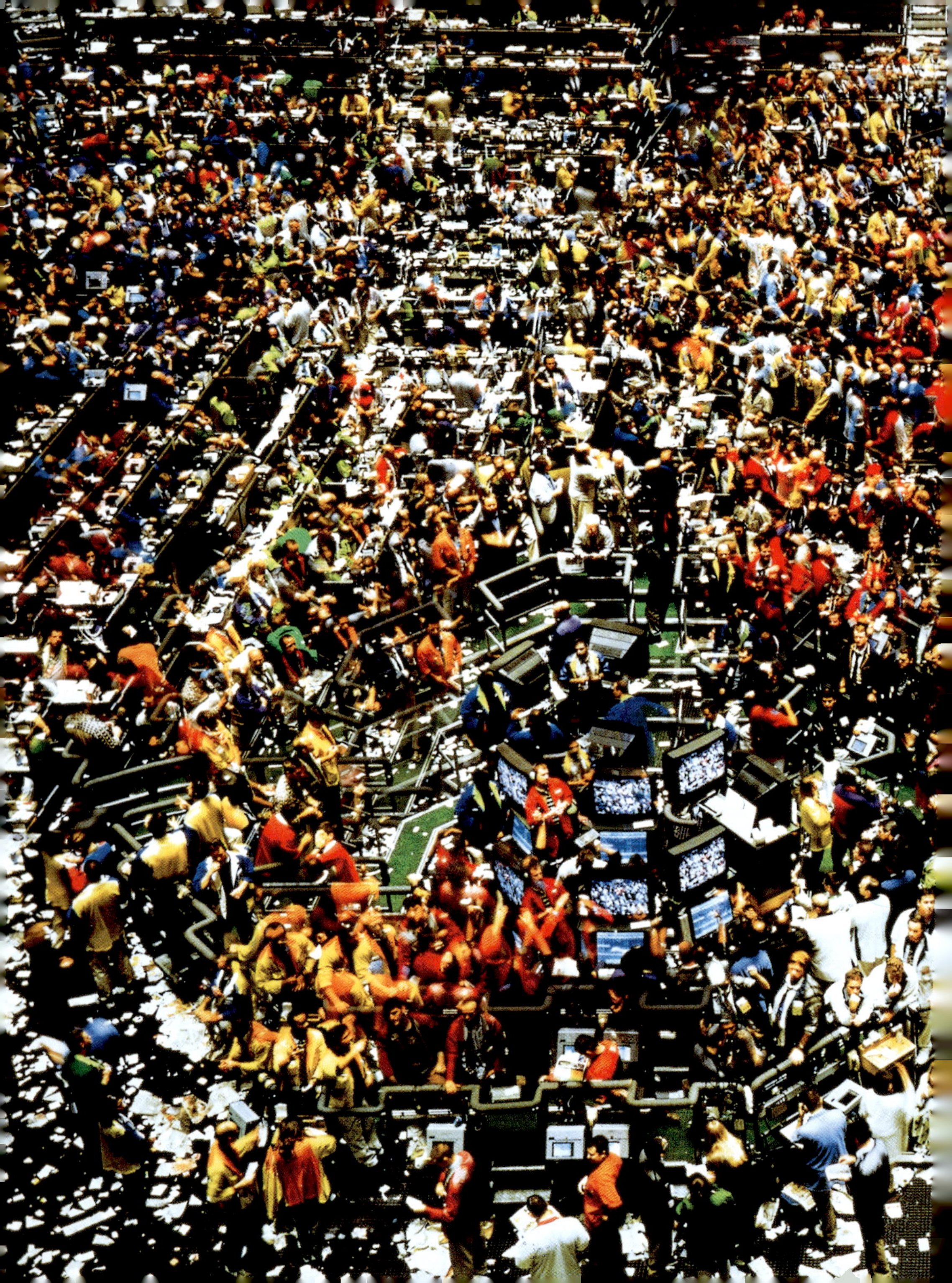

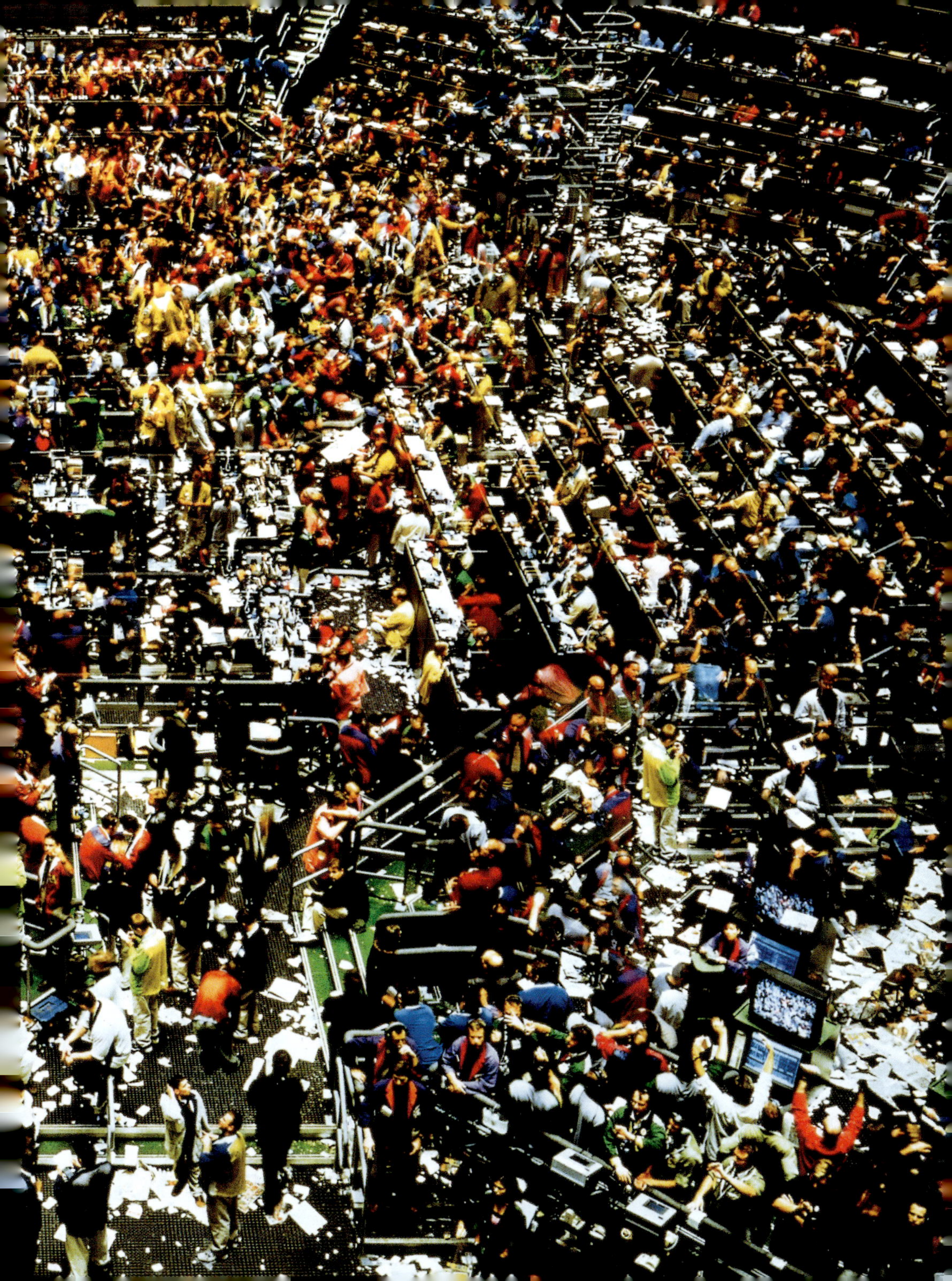

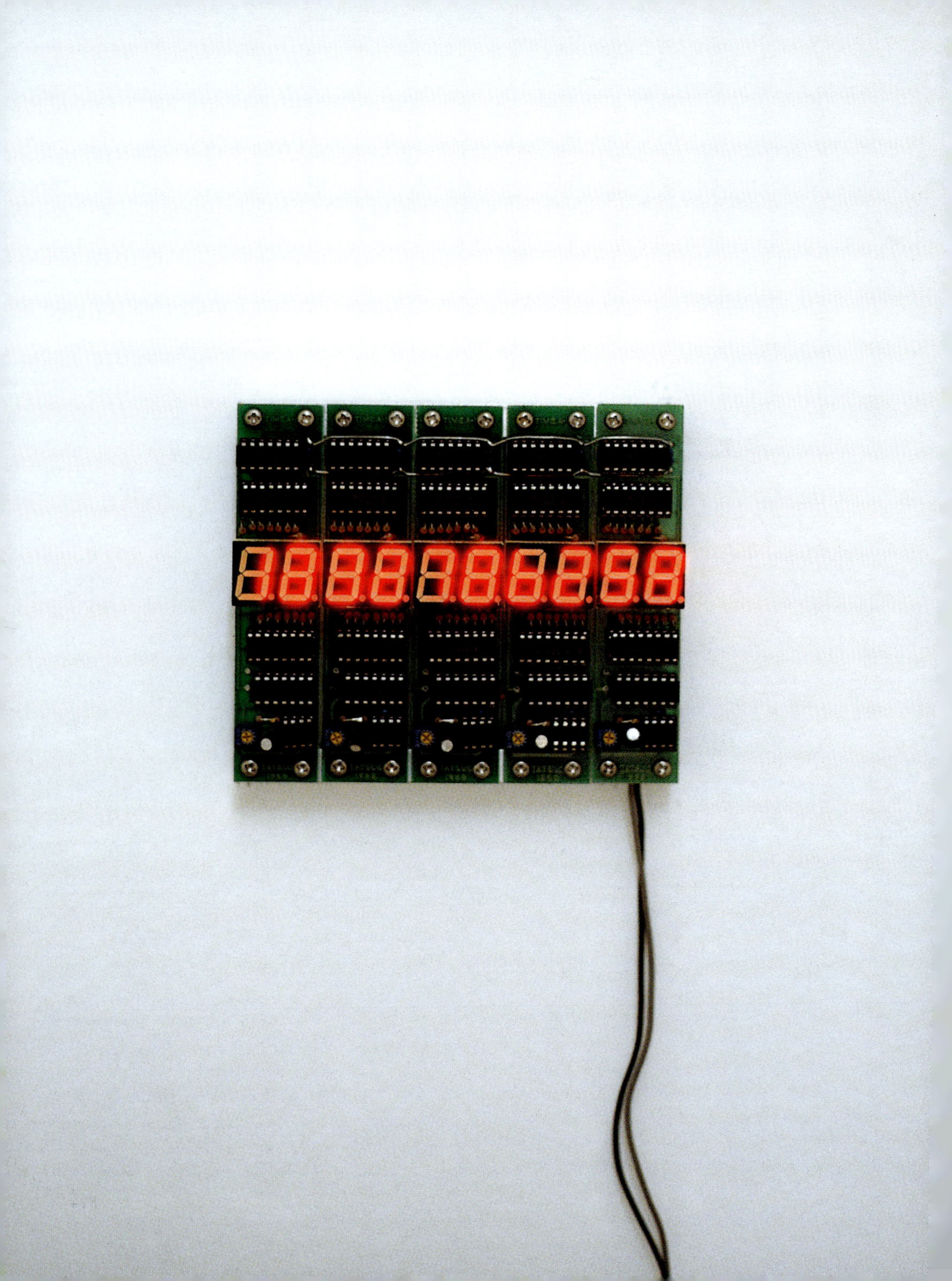

previous spread:
Chicago Board of Trade II
Andreas Gursky
1999

opposite:
Flextime/Coretime #7
Tatsuo Miyajima
1988

below:
Costa del Sol, 1996
photo Graham Gussin

overleaf:
Observatory
Catherine Yass
2000

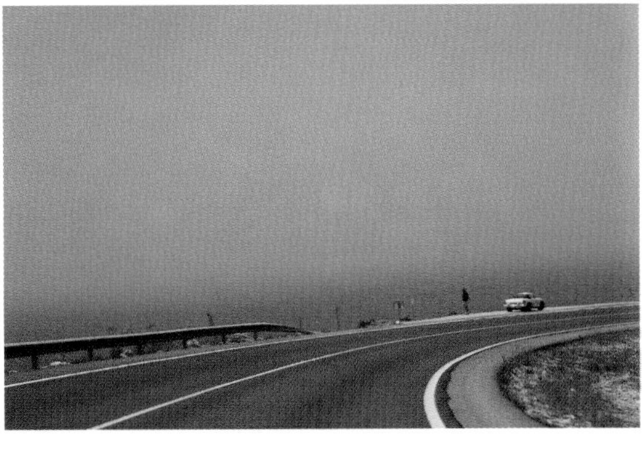

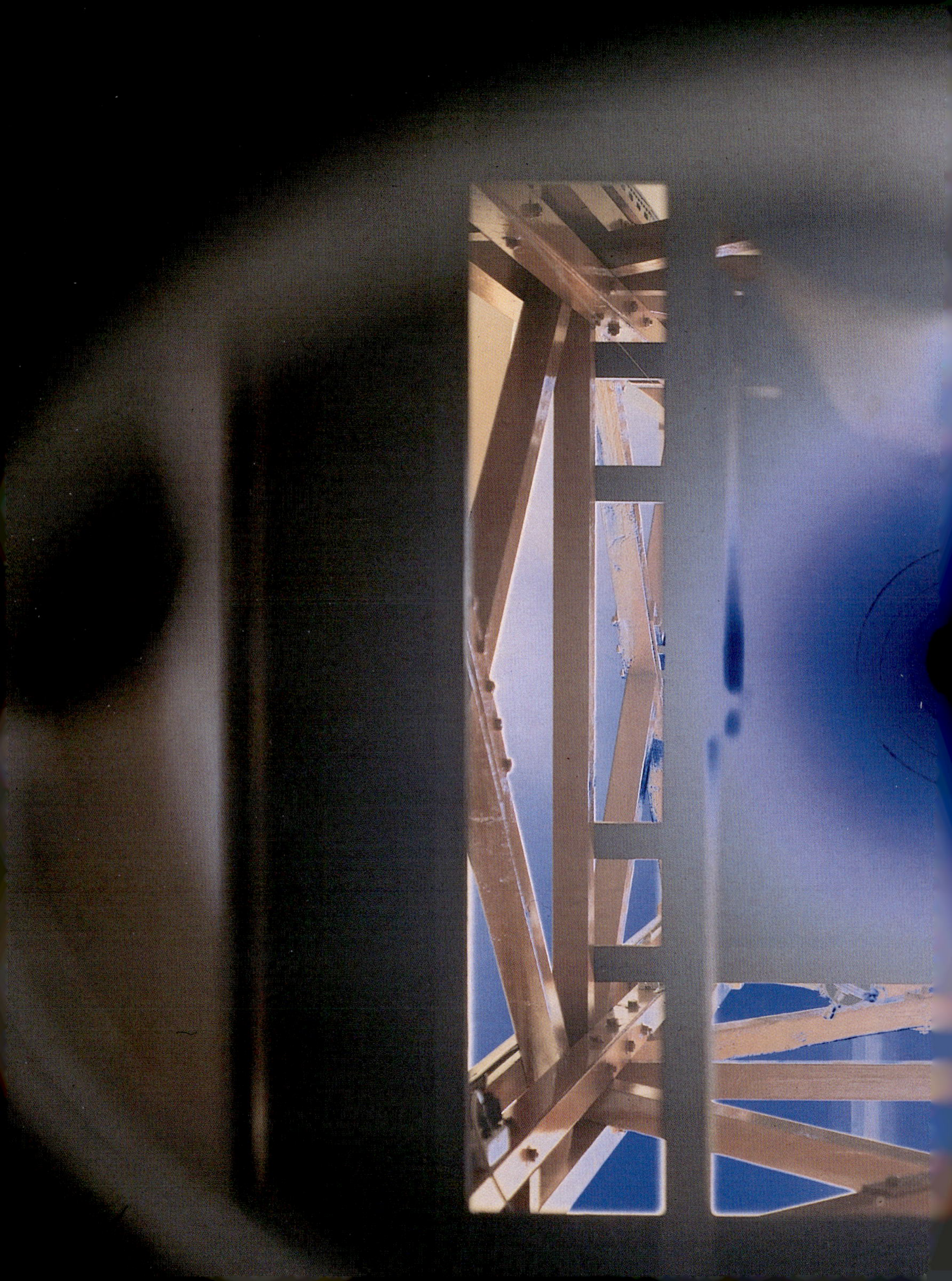

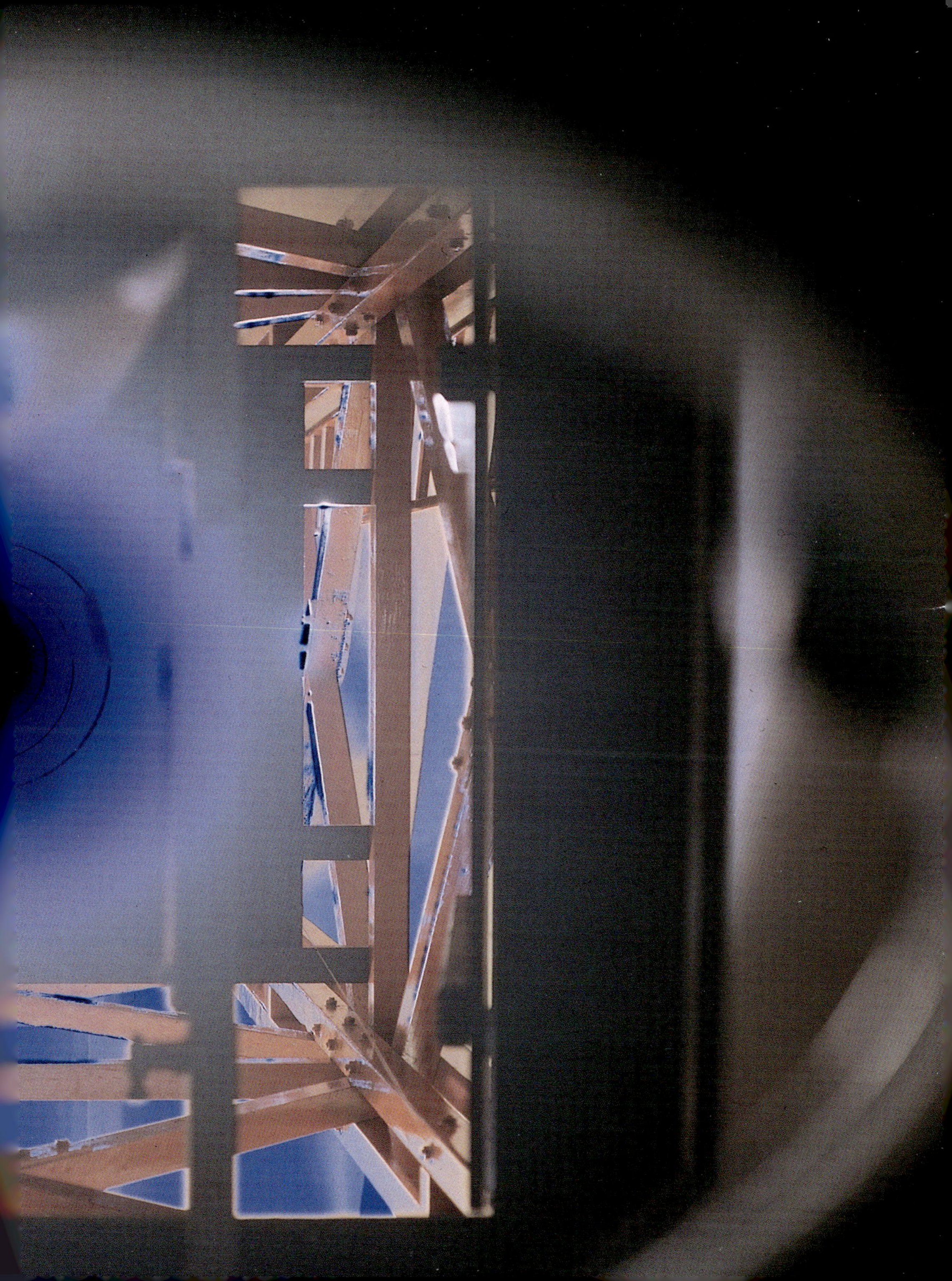

Report on an Unidentified Space Station
J G Ballard

SURVEY REPORT 1

By good luck we have been able to make an emergency landing on this uninhabited space station. There have been no casualties. We all count ourselves fortunate to have found safe haven at a moment when the expedition was clearly set on disaster.

The station carries no identification markings and is too small to appear on our charts. Although of elderly construction it is soundly designed and in good working order, and seems to have been used in recent times as a transit deposit for travellers resting at mid-point in their journeys. Its interior consists of a series of open passenger concourses, with comfortably equipped lounges and waiting rooms. As yet we have not been able to locate the bridge or control centre. We assume that the station was one of many satellite drogues surrounding a larger command unit, and was abandoned when a decline in traffic left it surplus to the needs of the parent transit system.

A curious feature of the station is its powerful gravitational field, far stronger than would be suggested by its small mass. However, this probably represents a faulty reading by our instruments. We hope shortly to complete our repairs and are grateful to have found shelter on this relic of the now forgotten migrations of the past.

Estimated diameter of the station: 500 metres.

SURVEY REPORT 2

Our repairs are taking longer than we first estimated. Certain pieces of equipment will have to be entirely rebuilt, and to shorten this task we are carrying out a search of our temporary home.

To our surprise we find that the station is far larger than we guessed. A thin local atmosphere surrounds the station, composed of interstellar dust attracted by its unusually high gravity. This fine vapour obscured the substantial bulk of the station and led us to assume that it was no more than a few hundred metres in diameter.

We began by setting out across the central passenger concourse that separates the two hemispheres of the station. This wide deck is furnished with thousands of tables and chairs. But on reaching the high partition doors 200 metres away we discovered that the restaurant deck is only a modest annexe to a far larger concourse. An immense roof three storeys high extends across an open expanse of lounges and promenades. We explored several of the imposing staircases, each equipped with a substantial mezzanine, and found that they lead to identical concourses above and below.

The space station has clearly been used as a vast transit facility, comfortably accommodating many thousands of passengers. There are now crew quarters or crowd control posts. The absence of even a single cabin indicates that this army of passengers spent only a brief time here before being moved on, and must have been remarkably self-disciplined or under powerful restraint.

Estimated diameter: 1 mile.

SURVEY REPORT 3

A period of growing confusion. Two of our number set out 48 hours ago to explore the lower decks of the station, and have so far failed to return. We have carried out an extensive search and fear that a tragic accident has taken place. None of the hundreds of elevators is in working order, but our companions may have entered an unanchored cabin and fallen to their deaths. We managed to force open one of the heavy doors and gazed with awe down the immense shaft. Many of the elevators within the station could comfortably carry a thousand passengers. We hurled several pieces of furniture down the shaft, hoping to time the interval before their impact, but not a sound returned to us. Our voices echoed away into a bottomless pit.

Perhaps our companions are marooned far from us on the lower levels? Given the likely size of the station, the hope remains that a maintenance staff occupies the crew quarters on some remote upper deck, unaware of our presence here.

Estimated diameter: 10 miles.

SURVEY REPORT 4

Once again our estimate of the station's size has been substantially revised. The station clearly has the dimensions of a large asteroid or even a small planet. Our instruments indicate that there are thousands of decks, each extending for miles across an undifferentiated terrain of passenger concourses, lounges and restaurant terraces. As before there is no sign of any crew or supervisory staff. Yet somehow a vast passenger complement was moved through this planetary waiting room.

While resting in the armchairs beneath the unvarying light we have all noticed how our sense of direction soon vanishes. Each of us sits at a point in space that at the same time seems to have no precise location but could be anywhere within these endless vistas of tables and armchairs. We can only assume that the passengers moving along these decks possessed some instinctive homing device, a mental model of the station that allowed them to make their way within it.

In order to establish the exact dimensions of the station and, if possible, rescue our companions we have decided to abandon our repair work and set out on an unlimited survey, however far this may take us.

Estimated diameter: 500 miles.

SURVEY REPORT 5

No trace of our companions. The silent interior spaces of the station have begun to affect our sense of time. We have been travelling in a straight line across one of the central decks for what seems an unaccountable period. The same pedestrian concourses, the same mezzanines attached to the stairways, and the same passenger lounges stretch for miles under an unchanging light. The energy needed to maintain this degree of illumination suggests that the operators of this station are used to a full passenger complement. However, there are unmistakable signs that no one has been here since the remote past.

We press on, following the same aisle that separates two adjacent lounge concourses. We rest briefly at fixed intervals, but despite our steady passage we sense that we are not moving at all, and may well be trapped within a small waiting room whose apparently infinite dimensions we circle like ants on a sphere. Paradoxically, our instruments confirm that we are penetrating a structure of rapidly increasing mass.

Is the entire universe no more than an infinitely vast space terminal?

Estimated diameter: 5,000 miles.

SURVEY REPORT 6

We have just made a remarkable discovery! Our instruments have detected that a slight but perceptible curvature is built into the floors of the station. The ceilings recede behind us and dip fractionally towards the decks below, while the disappearing floors form a distinct horizon.

So the station is a curvilinear structure of finite form! There must be meridians that mark out its contours, and an equator that will return us to our original starting point. We all feel an immediate surge of hope. Already we may have stumbled on an equatorial line, and despite the huge length of our journey we may in fact be going home.

Estimated diameter: 50,000 miles.

SURVEY REPORT 7

Our hopes have proved to be short-lived. Excited by the thought that we had mastered the station, and cast a net around its invisible bulk, we are pressing on with renewed confidence. However, we now know that although these curvatures exist, they extend in all directions. Each of the walls curves away from its neighbours, the floors from the ceilings. The station, in fact, is an expanding structure whose size appears to increase exponentially. The longer the journey undertaken by a passenger, the greater the incremental distance he will have to travel. The virtually unlimited facilities of the station suggest that its passengers embarked on extremely long, if not infinite journeys.

Needless to say, the complex architecture of the station has ominous implications for us. We realise that the size of the station is a measure, not of the numbers of passengers embarked – though this must have been vast – but of the length of the journeys undertaken within it. Indeed, there should ideally be only one passenger. A solitary voyager embarked on an infinite journey would require an infinity of transport lounges. As there are, fortunately, more than one of us we can assume that the station is a finite structure with the appearance of an infinite one. The degree to which it approaches an infinite size is merely a measure of the will and ambition of its passengers.

Estimated diameter: 1 million miles.

SURVEY REPORT 8

Just when our spirits were at their lowest ebb we have made a small but significant finding. We were moving across one of the limitless passenger decks, a prey to all fears and speculations, when we noticed the signs of recent habitation. A party of travellers has passed here in the recent past. The chairs in the central concourse have been disturbed, an elevator door has been forced, and there are the unmistakable traces left by weary voyagers. Without doubt there were more than two of them, so we must regretfully exclude our lost companions.

But there are others in the station, perhaps embarked on a journey as endless as our own!

We have also noticed slight variations in the decor of the station, in the design of light fittings and floor tiles. These may seem trivial, but multiplying them by the virtually infinite size of the station we can envisage a gradual evolution in its architecture. Somewhere in the station there may well be populated enclaves, even entire cities, surrounded by empty passenger decks that stretch on forever like free space. Perhaps there are nation-states whose civilisations rose and declined as their peoples paused in their endless migrations across the station.

What force propelled them on their meaningless journeys? We can only hope that they were driven forward by the greatest of all instincts, the need to establish the station's size.

Estimated diameter: 5 light years.

SURVEY REPORT 9

We are jubilant! A growing euphoria has come over us as we move across these great concourses. We have seen no further trace of our fellow passengers, and it now seems likely that we were following one of the inbuilt curvatures of the station and had crossed our own tracks.

But this small setback counts for nothing now. We have accepted the limitless size of the station, and this awareness fills us with feelings that are almost religious. Our instruments confirm what we have long suspected, that the empty space across which we travelled from our own solar system in fact lies within the interior of the station, one of the many vast lacunae set in its endlessly curving walls. Our solar system and its planets, the millions of other solar systems that constitute our galaxy, and the island universes themselves all lie within the boundaries of the station. Our duty is to travel across it in on a journey whose departure point we have already begun to forget, and whose destination is the station itself, every floor and concourse within it.

So we move on, sustained by our faith in the station, aware that every step we take thereby allows us to reach a small part of that destination. By its existence the station sustains us, and gives our lives their only meaning. We are glad that in return we have to begun to worship the station.

Estimated diameter: 15 million light years.

overleaf left:
Photograph taken inside the CERN particle accelerator

overleaf right:
Work No.141
Martin Creed
1995

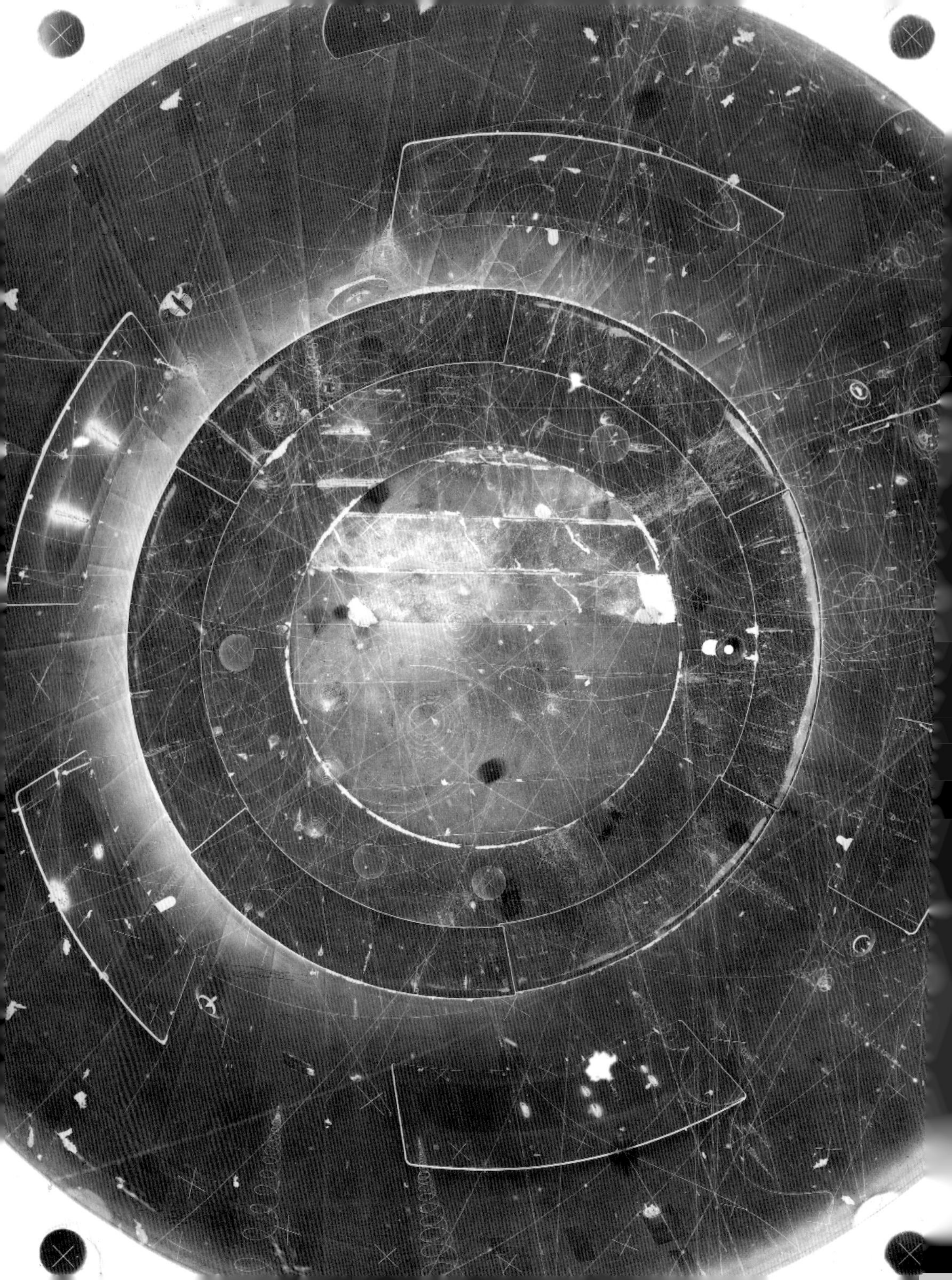

from none
take one
add one
make none

Map of a thirty-six square mile surface area of the Pacific Ocean west of Oahu

Scale 3 inches : 1 mile

THIS SURFACE CONSTITUTES A DRAWING THAT WILL BE COMPLETED AFTER ITS PERCIPIENT HAS:

LOOKED AT IT
BREATHED TOWARD IT
READ THESE WORDS
FORGOTTEN THEM

previous spread, left:
Map of a thirty-six square mile surface area of the Pacific Ocean west of Oahu
Art & Language
1967

previous spread, right:
Untitled
Douglas Huebler
1969

below:
Anechoic chamber
(the National Physical Laboratory, Teddington)

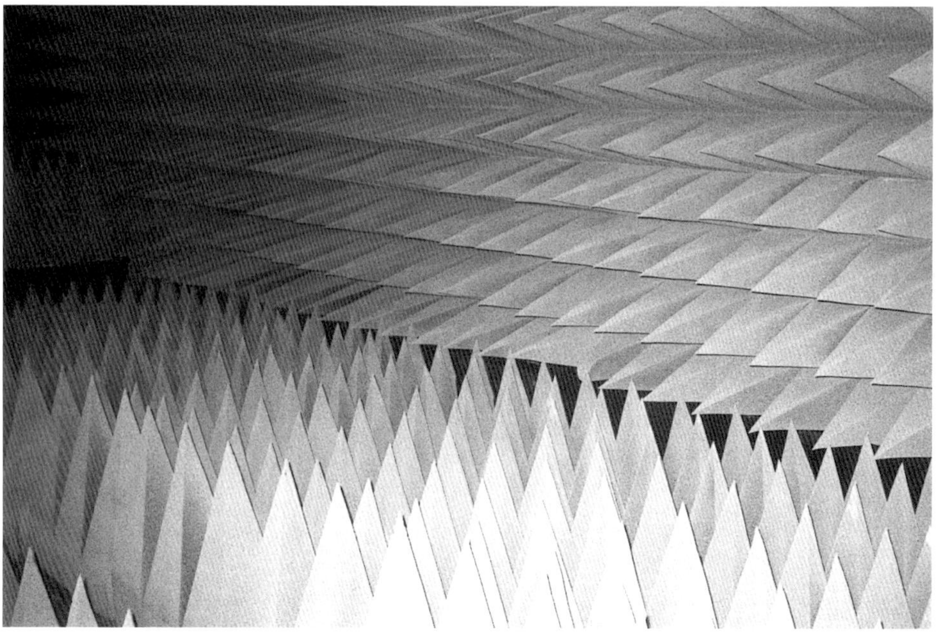

A note on corporate identity olfactory chemicals

Smell is a sensory perception which is often targetted in public environments such as airports, museums and shopping areas. Companies such as British Airways and attractions like the Millennium Dome use olfactory properties in their corporate design schemes. As environmental sound systems have been designed to stimulate worker productivity and consumer behaviour in the past, research with smell has increasingly begun to explore the genetic basis of neurological cognition. Placed in ventilation systems, these chemicals are configured by their manufacturers to connote adjectives like 'sophistication', 'dependability' and 'freshness'.

Sean Snyder

Nothing, Apocalypse and Utopia
Charles Gere

One of the most forceful images of nothing, *Mother of God*, was created by Robert Rauschenberg in 1950. In the centre of the image is a pure white circle covering a collage of maps of a city. The work is a meditation on the likely effects of nuclear conflict, in which human life and culture (here represented by the maps and the city they delineate), are annihilated, literally reduced to nothing. From this point, Rauschenberg went on to paint his series of all-white and all-black paintings, in which the idea of emptiness and nothing was developed and explored more emphatically. At first, it might seem that such a move was a nihilistic gesture, celebrating only the hopelessness and despair engendered by the Cold War and the prospect of nuclear war, as well as the more general and diffuse sense of despair felt by many in the post-war period.

Yet these apparently bleak representations of nothing actually contain a powerful utopian charge. This was perceived by Rauschenberg's friend, avant-garde composer, John Cage. Cage realised that far from being empty, the paintings, by virtue of their being surfaces on which dust or shadows may settle, were in fact full of action and interest. As well as by Rauschenberg's work, Cage was also inspired by his visit to the entirely soundproof anechoic chamber at Harvard, where, hoping to experience silence, he was overwhelmed by the noise of his own body; the beating of his heart and the rushing of blood demonstrated that such a proposition was impossible.

This realisation gave Cage 'permission' to compose *4'33"*, the piece of silent music that he had long been contemplating. It was premiered in 1952 in Woodstock, upstate New York, in a now legendary performance by pianist David Tudor. In accordance with Cage's 'Tacet' instructions, Tudor sat at the piano without playing, for three 'movements' which in total lasted the four minutes and thirty-three seconds of the piece's title. Despite Cage referring to it as his 'silent piece', *4'33"* is not about silence at all, but rather about its impossibility. It makes the audience listen to the ordinary ambient noises which they would otherwise ignore and treat them with the respect usually granted to music.

This is more than a provocative musical gesture. Whether or not Cage intended it as such, *4'33"* is a profoundly utopian statement that repudiates the nihilism implicit in emptiness; instead, it treats it as a space in which anything and everything is possible – any noise and all noises become music. This notion is as relevant and necessary now as it was then. In the early 1950s, Cage's silence offered a sense of possibility to counter the seeming inevitability of nuclear holocaust. Fifty years later, as that threat has (apparently) receded, *4'33"* suggests that there are possibilities other than those which form a part of the relentless onward march of technologised capital towards global dominance.

overleaf:
Steam (second version)
Robert Morris
1974

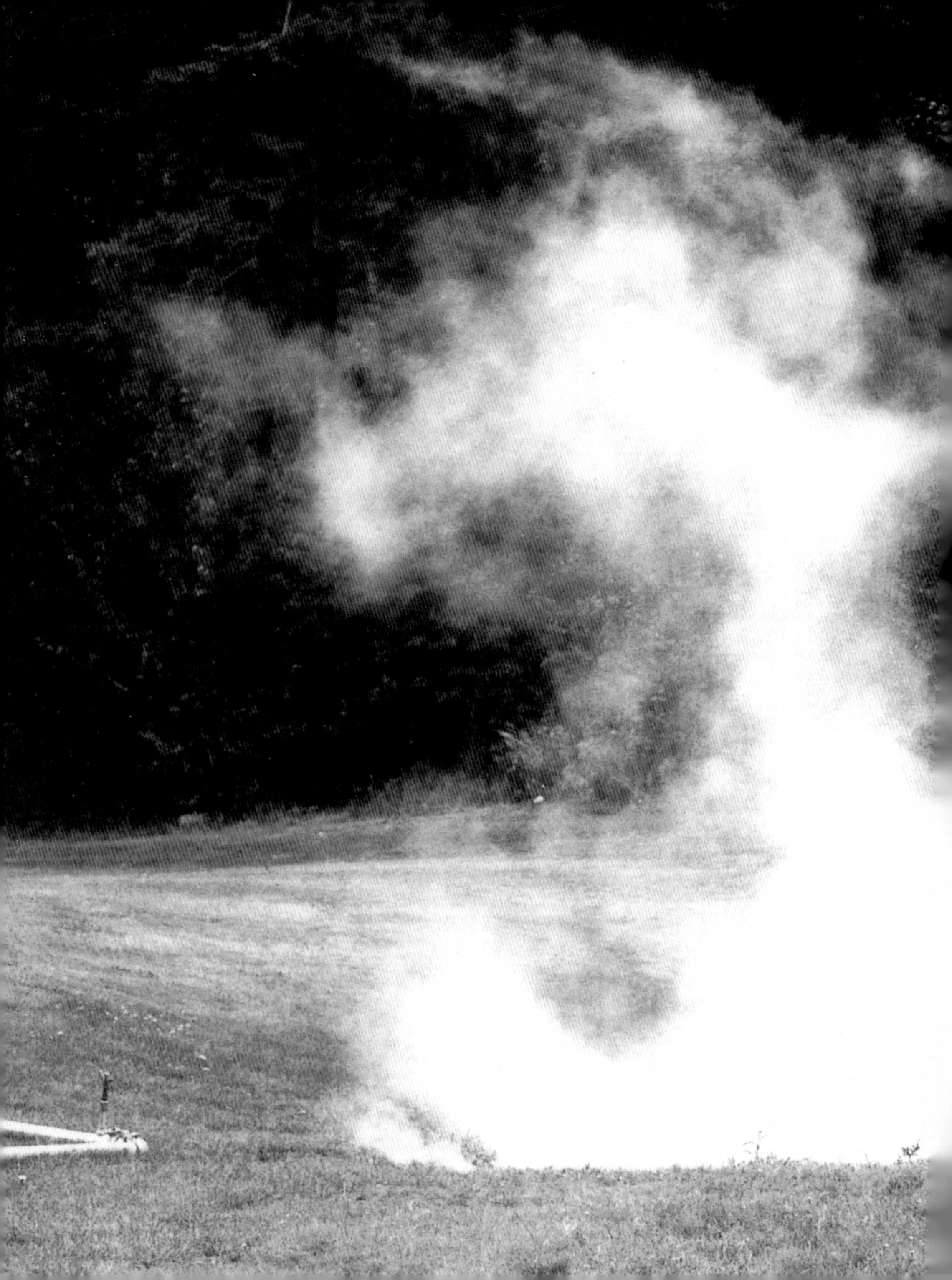

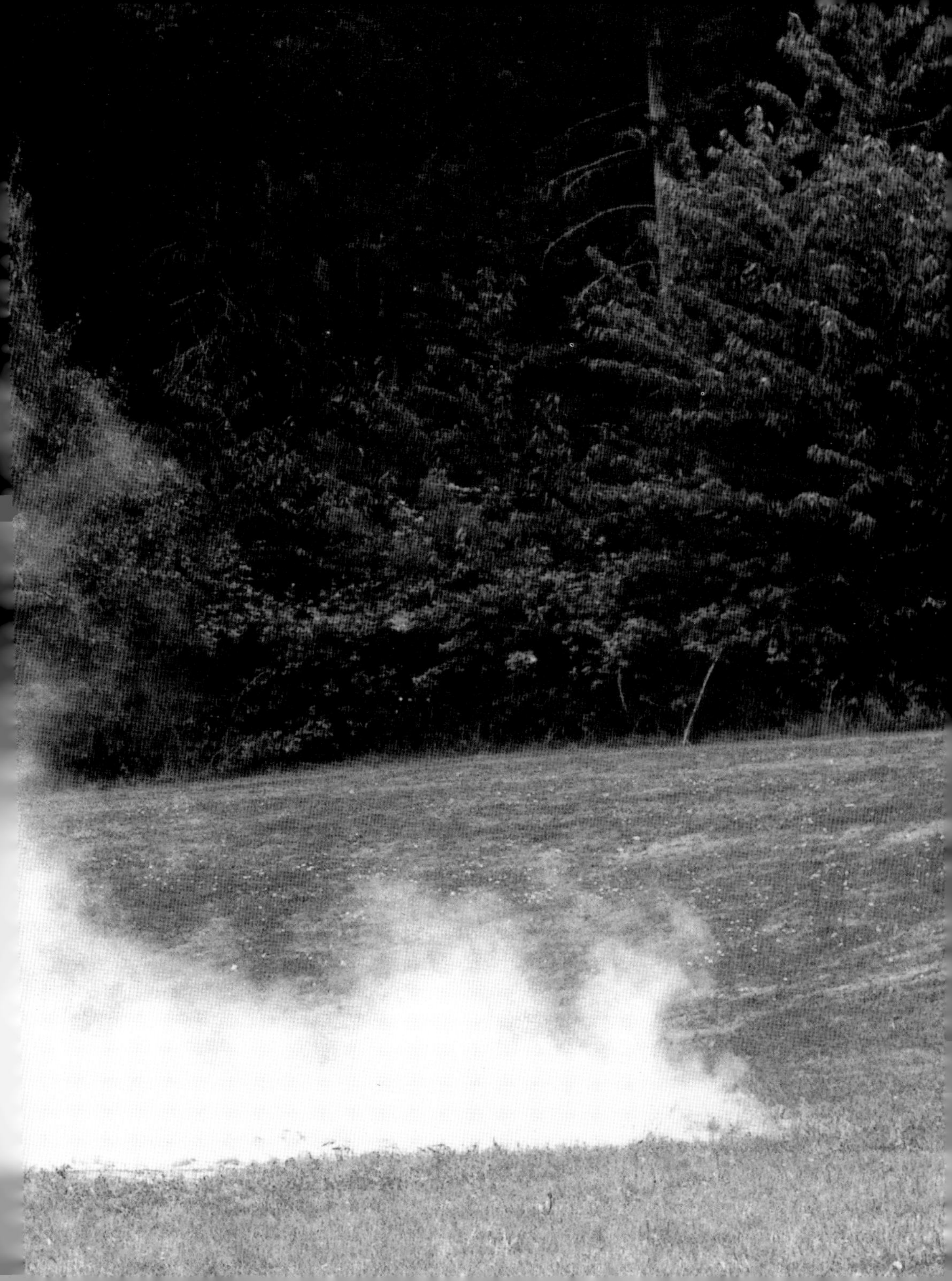

Is It Out There?
Robert Kaplan

Nature abhors a vacuum and so do we. Zero, we've seen, is intricately woven into the workings of our thought, but the temptation time and again has been to look for its original outside of the mind, in physical space: a silent desert amid the clamour of oases. We may be disappointed. Like those cartographers in the Age of Discovery who filled up the vacant corners of their maps with winds and serpents, and wrote over still unexplored regions, 'Here be Monsters', the cosmologists who are our modern navigators of stellar immensity posit brief surges of energy and fleeting bursts of quasi-quanta where you might have thought nothing was happening and there wasn't anything for it to happen to.

Just as our emptiest rooms turn out to be dense with invisible radiation (you have only to tune in the appropriate receiver – radio, television – to make it appear), so the light of a billion stars, the background hum from the Big Bang and ever fainter echoes of countless pasts are expanding through one another everywhere, making the hollow night claustrophobic. Even if you speak not in terms of the something of energy but the something of substance and ask: must there not be a place – numberless places – where there is no matter at all? – you will hear a dusty reply from our cosmologists. Empty space itself, theory suggests and measurement indirectly confirms, is a lusty begetter of virtual particles: for mirroring the rivalry in mathematics between continuous and discrete approaches to zero, theories of space seem to oscillate between an energised vacuum and a sea of all but things.

So when the orthodox theory of ether held sway (the theory that explained light as waves in an all-pervasive, rarefied fluid), you would have expected – given the pushmi-pullyu of fashion – that a contrary hypothesis would have arisen which filled up space with celestial ball-bearings: and you would have been right. In that corner of the library where no young and hardly any old codgers go are stored the books of yesterday's certainties, the delicate charm of their fustiness ruffled only by the ever modern authority of their tone. Here you will find – almost invisibly wedged away – Osborne Reynolds's slim volume, *On an Inversion of Ideas as to the Structure of the Universe*.

Its date is 1903 and its writer – an English professor of engineering – assures us that we may have the fullest confidence in his explanations, whose success will achieve 'that ideal which, from the time of Thales and Plato, has excited the highest philosophical interest'. The reason for his confidence is that his 'inversion of ideas' perfectly explains, he says, the basic phenomena of physics (the absorption and reflection of light, gravitation, etc.), and 'Considering that not one of these phenomena had previously received a mechanical explanation, it appears how indefinitely small' (zero à la mode) 'must be the probability that there should be another structure for the universe which would satisfy the same evidence.'

And what is his explanation? Why, that there is no empty space, but that the universe is all compact of inconceivably small grains (their diameters are the seven hundred thousand millionth part of the wave-length of violet light), moving at about one and one-third feet per second relative to one another, along very short paths. They make up an elastic medium that extends to infinity, and in their piling account for everything we know. Well may Reynolds ask: 'Could anything be more simple?' His theory explains, for example, why the sky is black on a clear night: the motion of light is dissipated to increase the relative motions of the grains. It accounts for gravitation as the result of the particles no longer being closely packed, due to inward strains. It even explains what we are: waves in this granular universe; '…that is what the singular surfaces, which we call matter, are – waves. We are all waves.'

O Archimedes, this is wondrous strange! Where are your poppy-seeds, and Buddha, your motes that danced in a sunbeam, now? A universe in which the void has disappeared – and not only the void, but Osborne Reynolds too: 'I have in my hand,' he writes, 'the first experimental model universe, a soft indiarubber bag…' And there is a photograph, his Figure 9, of the universe (marked W) gripped in a hand that extends from a white cuff, itself shot from a dark sleeve. But the photograph ends before the elbow. There is no more. It is the only likeness I have of Osborne Reynolds and his universe.

A quarter century later, when quantum mechanics was carrying all before it, another inversion of ideas gave us positively charged particles as holes in a universal, undetectable sea of negativity. This was PAM Dirac's way of saving the fundamental wave equation that bears his name, and which describes how electrons move, from some very nasty consequences (such as electrons growing ever more negative and radiating away infinite amounts of energy as they did so). It was a solution – as one physicist put it –'that made up in brilliance what it lacked in plausibility', and there is certainly something to be said for seeing the positive as a zero in negative contexts. Dirac's sea, however, went the way of Reynolds's shore when the negative energy solutions were later rethought as positive energy states of a different particle.

Now, as we understand it, the deepest freeze in the uttermost basements of space is around 2.7 degrees above absolute zero, signalling the presence there of something in motion. More (or less, since less is more): even a vacuum empty of all matter is still a surging ocean of energy in the form of fluctuating electromagnetic waves, as shown by their exerting a force on uncharged plates (a prediction made in 1948 by the Dutch physicist Hendrick Casimir and finally confirmed in 1996 at Los Alamos). The amount of this 'vacuum energy' is (troublingly) infinite, according to current theory; but thus far only the little people in flying saucers seem able to tap it.

If we aren't to find nothingness in the great open spaces, what about the minute closed ones we make at home, under the bell jar? In 1670 Robert Boyle, the English chemist and alchemist – founder with his fellow natural philosophers of a society they called the Invisible College – put a bird in a glass and pumped out the air. You see it fluttering still in the painting Joseph Wright of Derby made a hundred years later: the little girl of the family turns away weeping; her brother pulls up the empty cage on a pulley; the adults stare at one another, at the experiment or into their thoughts – only the flowing-haired figure at the apparatus looks out at us with tense inquiry, and we look riveted back.

'Is it enough?' he seems to be asking. Yes, as far as killing the bird goes; no, if he wanted a perfect vacuum. Generations of quiet, ingenious workers have brought us much closer. You wouldn't guess, passing them in the street outside their laboratories, that to them the world is well lost for one more zero in the decimal perfecting of their results. They live their work: William Fairbank – long the doyen of near-zero researchers – slept with his windows open to frigid winds and dusted the snow from his bedding in the morning.

These days physicists use lasers to stop rubidium atoms dead in their tracks and so super-cool them in an evacuated glass thermos, then trigger a magnetic trap to cool them further, to within 100 billionths of a degree of absolute zero. At this point those atoms act collectively as one; yet even were their temperature precisely zero they would, paradoxically, have not quite zero energy. This follows from quantum mechanics, at whose core lies Heisenberg's Uncertainty Principle, which says that when it comes to an electron, you can at any moment know where it is or how fast it is moving, but not both – but you would be pardoned for thinking that rather the principles of Mahāvīrā's syādvāda were central here, and this all but empty world of minute appearances was at the same time real, unreal and indescribable.

Following Kant, it is clear that we can imagine space without objects but never objects without space. But modern physics at its macroscopic and microscopic extremes seems to have shown that we cannot think of actual space as empty. Doesn't its bending around to cradle galaxies, its acting as a matrix for particles spurting into and out of existence, accord well with our revised understanding of the Hindu void, śūnya, not as empty but pregnant?

If we seek a simpler, purer zero out there, we may have to look for it in a different guise. What about the *mass* of certain particles? Some physicists are sure that speaking of a photon's or a graviton's mass is meaningful, and that this mass is zero – but it isn't anything they can prove.

Turn then to what surely has a zero stamped on it: time, which of all things best deserves to be called the unmoved mover. Yet here again we are likely to be frustrated: what we hear of the noise celebrating that first new year is a Big Bang after a few nanoseconds which, for all our ears and minds, we cannot recapture. Or was it more than a nest of instants – did billions of years or even an infinite stretch of time precede the birth of our universe?

For the cosmological theory we've been soldiering along with over the decades is in crisis: recalcitrant facts are breaking it up into almost as many patchwork hypotheses as the universes some think are jostling one another, mere bubbles in a beery froth. Perhaps it is about to be downed by a despondent medical student named Prior, as John Collier's story, 'The Devil, George and Rosie', explains. Don't worry, the Devil says: '… it will be twenty million billion years before his lips reach the glass, for a young woman is fixing him with her eye, and by the time he drinks all the bubbles will be gone…'

Some cosmologists give time no beginning, some would have it perceived differently within and outside a bubble universe, some see our particular bubble's time as linear within the larger universe's cyclic time, and yet others picture it 'before' the Big Bang as behaving like space, with no headlong direction. These scenarios follow from the varied ways of rejigging a derelict theory to fit new observations. They make you marvel once again at the power of language and abstraction, since time seems so much a condition of all our doing that you wonder where you must stand to see it thus from afar. Time, to paraphrase Kant, is something we think with, hence only perilously about.

Could we find zero perhaps in a cogent answer to the related question: what did the world begin *with*? Here too there are numerous knockers at the gate. One physicist says: 'The reason that there is Something rather than Nothing is that Nothing is unstable.'

St Augustine wrestled hard and long with this problem in his *Confessions*, all too aware that our questions outpace our answers and that many different senses can and ought to be extracted from a text. He concluded that the earth and the deep, which in the beginning were invisible and lightless and without form, God must have made from almost nothing, *prope nihil*: '… not altogether nothing; for there was a certain formlessness, without any beauty'. A wonderfully subtle position to take, by a man whose thought has so informed ours. Should we therefore be surprised to find how similar the view is sixteen centuries later? As the universe cooled after the Big Bang, matter and anti-matter almost annihilated one another, to leave pure radiation. The symmetry wasn't perfect, however (it was without any beauty): for every hundred million pairs of quarks and anti-quarks there was one extra quark, the foundation of matter – and this faintest tip of the balance evolved to stars and planets and seagulls and ourselves.

The ends of space and the beginnings of time: it turns out zero wasn't crouching in either of these trees we have been barking up. More natural, surely, to look for it out there at the dead centre of things. That was how zero came to be understood as the negative numbers grew increasingly vivid: the fulcrum they and the positives balanced around; and, more broadly, as the linchpin of coordinate systems that let us navigate safely out and back again.

Where is this centre? Zeus found it by starting two eagles at the same moment from the eastern and western edges of the world: they met at Delphi, and the sacred stone there marks the world's omphalos. Might that stone – or navels in general – have contributed to the form of zero, accounting perhaps in particular for the peculiar ⊙ we met in medieval times? Long after Zeus, Aristotle took the Pythagoreans to task for putting the sun at the centre of the universe on purely theoretical grounds (fire, being superior to earth, they said, deserved the honour). His observations led him to affirm what most knew, that the earth was at the centre – where it remained for many centuries.

The centre of this centre was called by early Muslim astronomers 'the cupola of the earth' – by the Hindus, the island of Lanka, their 0° longitude and (charmingly) without latitude. It was there that the demon Râvana built the labyrinthine fortress Yâvana-koti, whose plan is strongly reminiscent of the palace made by the sons of Atlas in Plato's Atlantis. But Atlantis sank beneath the ocean for its sins, and there is no such cupola, said the traveler Albīrūnī a millennium ago, while Lanka he guessed to be the cannibal island Langa, source of cloves and the wind that brought small-pox.

Even the notion of the earth as midmost of all came under a series of diverse and remarkable attacks before Copernicus dealt it a lethal blow in 1560. The Stoics, for example, in the generations following Aristotle, saw the material universe afloat in an infinite void. The former might have a centre but the whole clearly could not. Long after, near the end of the Middle Ages, the Cardinal of Brixen, Nicolaus Cusanus, claimed that the physical universe was by its very nature imprecise, so that neither the earth nor the world itself could be a true sphere since a more perfect one was always possible. Being indefinite, therefore, none had a centre. In fact the true centre of the universe, he said, coincides with its circumference and neither is physical: that perfection belongs alone to God. Because no mortal can be at this centre, all of our differing views are equivalent – and equivalently lacking in objectivity:

> Combine thus these diverse imaginations... and then, with the intellect, which alone can practice *learned ignorance*, you will see that the world and its motion cannot be represented by a figure, because it will appear almost as a wheel within a wheel, and a sphere within a sphere, having nowhere, as we have seen, either a centre or a circumference.

If you want to take in at a glance how the centre of western thought shifted over five turbulent centuries, just compare three treatments of this metaphor, with that of Cusanus acting as their mean. The first is from the twelfth-century *Book of the XXIV Philosophers*, where God is described as a

> *Sphaera cuius centrum ubique, circumferentia nullibi:*

a sphere whose centre is everywhere, its circumference nowhere.

The passage quoted before from Cusanus, written in 1440, continues:

> It is as if the machine of this world had its centre everywhere and its circumference nowhere, because the circumference and the centre are God, who is everywhere and nowhere.

By 1660 only the machine is left. Pascal writes in his *Pensées*:

> The whole visible world... is an infinite sphere, the centre of which is everywhere, the circumference nowhere.

So we pass from a finite, through an indefinite, to an infinite universe.

With Copernicus the centre contracted to the sun, and there it still was fifty years later for Kepler, and for Newton later still. Between them, Galileo was cautiously sceptical: 'We do not know where to find the centre of the universe or whether it exists at all.' Since it was politically incorrect to express such doubts (and metaphysical scandals then carried far heavier penalties than physical scandals now) – and perhaps because Galileo saw no way to test them – he left the question alone.

Not so Leibniz, who carried his attack on Newton into space. For Newton, space was the shining frame which made sense of the

relations among bodies within it; for Leibniz, space was just the order of these related bodies and wouldn't exist without them. Unlike the two women shouting from their Edinburgh windows at one another, who would never agree (says Sydney Smith) because they were arguing from different premises, Newton and Leibniz would never agree because their premises were the same: God needed the greatest glorification. Absolute, empty space, Newton thought, implied God's continual governance of all within it; this read, to Leibniz, as God always having to wind up a faltering clock.

The arguments themselves wound up and down, changing terms, tropes and proponents – then were swept away at a stroke two hundred years later by Einstein. For Leibniz saw that Newton had conjured up absolute space in order to talk (as in his First Law) about absolute motion in it; but that no such motion could ever be observed, since you would detect no change – hence the fiction of absolute space was unnecessary. Einstein stood this remark on its head: what one observed from, he realised, are private frames of reference, each bearing its own centre, its zero, about with it. As long as the frames were unmoving, or moved uniformly with respect to one another, each would appear at rest to its occupant, and while events seen from them would be measured as occurring at different times and places to different observers, the laws governing the events – the laws of physics – would read as indistinguishably the same. This was Einstein's Principle of Relativity, which thus neither affirmed nor denied the notion of an absolute space with a fixed centre, but made it meaningless.

Has this parade of just a few rival cosmologies made you doubt cosmology altogether, or suspect it to be an annex of theology? Do you worry that this science harbours its own Uncertainty Principle which lets us determine either what a position is or how fast it is changing? The difficulty lies in trying to sketch out the universe by connecting too few datum-points. Does the last elephant holding the universe up stand on a turtle, or is it elephants all the way down? For despite the confidence of Osborne Reynolds, any number of interpretations will be consistent with a limited body of evidence. Which theories arise and thrive may involve something more than how well they fit their curves to the facts. If the temper of the times is aesthetic, elegance outranks sheer plod, and brilliance more than makes up for plausibility. Even the leisure pursuits of a critical community may incline its science toward hypotheses that resonate with science fiction.

More fundamentally, when at the very edge of your territory (and it is always on the edge that science moves) you may believe as settlers do that the world afar is like the world at hand, and so strive for analytic continuations of known laws into that unknown; or like an explorer you may seek to distance yourself from a provincial past, rejoicing in the essentially singular. Nothing new under the sun? Then beyond it! And while we are all over-reachers on a negligible speck of dust, cosmologists among us seem to belong to the second camp.

Yet settler or explorer, they are scientists in the end rather than theologians – and rather than literary critics. They read the book of nature without benefit of old or new criticism, semiotics or structuralism, believing what as humans they can't help but believe, that what is out there is unequivocal and – unlike scripture – independent of our interpretations. Their ends may be hubristic but their means are modest, and in their mind's eye they still wear the white lab coats of the objective, detached observer. Not for them the truth of formalised mathematics that there are essentially different models of the same phenomena: they resemble the mathematicians inventing rather than validating relations, and recognising with a shock that these inventions are discoveries within the singular way things are.

Why, then, is cosmology's evolution punctuated rather than continuous? Because there is – as William Whewell said some hundred and fifty years ago – a mask of theory over the whole face of nature. It is this mask scientists look at, rather than through: a mask of papier-mâché, pasted together from fragmentary facts that compile to features so far from those they first crudely conformed to. It is a mask whose layers crack and peel apart when its flour-and-water reasoning dries out.

Yet zeroes like eye-holes pierce this mask in many places. We saw an instance before where they signalled the maxima and minima of processes. The deepest laws of physics are written in what Napier, you remember, called 'equations to nothing': those laws of conservation, I mean, that say the total energy (or charge, or momentum or matter) in a system remains the same: its changes amount to exchanges that sum to zero. These laws go back at least as far as Descartes, who held that what God created He then preserved. Although the objects that physics studies variously altered or grew more precise and even multiplied over time, the laws expressing their conservation were themselves conserved. These laws and their ilk aren't decorative incisings on the pillars holding up our understanding of the world: they are the stuff of the least brick, alone letting us build a detailed image in the likeness of things – half of whose texture is therefore these zeroes.

A telling example: it may not be all that easy to study the forces poised in bodies (such as a system of pulleys) at rest – in equilibrium – but it is a great deal easier than analysing those of bodies in motion (swinging, sliding, rotating, rebounding, falling). Any way of reducing such dynamics to the former statics would clearly be welcomed. This is just what Jean Le Rond d'Alembert did in 1743 – and did by a change so slight in the mere *form* of an equation that we relish anew the power of grammar to yield insight (which, like faith, follows from just going on tinkering).

For Newton's Second Law of *Motion* asserts that moving force is the same as the mass of the body moved times its acceleration:

$$F = ma.$$

This puts the three terms in a mutually defining dance that promises severe difficulties in analysing such forces. What d'Albembert did in effect was just to rewrite Newton's equation as

$$F - ma = 0,$$

then to consider the term '$-ma$' as itself a force, 'the force of inertia':

$I = -ma$. So now we have:

$$F + I = 0$$

But this states that the sum of the forces, F and I, produces equilibrium: and hence dynamics is reduced to statics. Of course equations with specific forces and 'forces of inertia' still have to be solved – but they can now be *understood* in the same way and from the same vantage point that familiar problems of equilibrium were.

Thus d'Alembert's Principle, that any system of forces is in equilibrium if we add together their applied and inertial varieties, has the character we recognised long since in double-entry bookkeeping: a balance is brought to zero with the aid of a little artifice. Magical helpers have magical helpers to help them.

You will rightly say of these conservation laws, as of d'Alembert's Principle, that being relations among things rather than things themselves they aren't truly out there, hence neither are the zeroes they involve. The virtual particles we began this chapter with are virtual not only in being taken almost as particles, but in being almost *taken*: for physicists take them more as mathematical metaphors, aids to conception and computation, very much like the infinitesimals of calculus that help us determine the slope of a curve at a point on it, but disappear once the calculation is done. Shall we temper Leibniz's claim that only individuals are real and relations belong fully to thought? Let's say instead that zero is a relation, and relations lie in that middle ground between mind and matter where mathematics strikes its accords, making interpretation and reality available to each other. Surely that is why these smaller-than-life figures of zero are always busy around the fringes of our affairs.

There they are on our thermometers, for example: but Fahrenheit was a man before he was a scale, choosing his zero as the lowest temperature attainable by a freezing mixture of ice and salt. René de Réaumur – when he wasn't studying the forms of birds' nests or proving that the strength of a rope was less than the combined strengths of its strands – argued for making zero the freezing point just of water. Anders Celsius observed the aurora in Lapland – well situated to devise the Centigrade zero; and William Thomson, Lord Kelvin, a blur of ceaseless calibrating the whole of his eighty-three years, set zero degrees as the temperature at which motion ceases.

Man is the measurer of all things. Look at the Plimsoll Line, there on ships the world over to save the lives of sailors by showing the level between safe and dangerous loading: Samuel Plimsoll came near to capsizing his own fortunes when he shook his fist in Disraeli's face and called his fellow members of Parliament villains for dropping the bill that would have outlawed the infamous 'coffin ships'. Look at our midnights, our meridians, look at what scales you will, they are all made with invented boundaries we almost believe are out there, but mark instead the personality of their inventors.

Still, might there not be a membrane of outside patterned with pores of zero – not as remote as the cosmos yet sufficiently far away to count as Out There? For we fall from time to time into Cartesian reveries where our bodies strike us as the bearers of what we are: inertial reference frames for the passenger mind. Professional athletes often talk of their accomplishments in this odd, third-personal way: evaluations of what the arms, the legs were up to, of a kind with racquet, ball, glove.

We often fail to savour to the full the astonishing virtuosity athletes show every day in diving for a ball and coming up throwing; in stretching for an overhead smash and landing ready for the return; in passing their centres of gravity smoothly under the bar they vault themselves over, or lithely leaning into and out of an ice-slick curve. Cat-like, they are geniuses at always having their bearings: a sensation we ourselves grow aware of in dancing, say, or cycling, and know without knowing through the thousand gestures of the day. Zero in the body as machine shows as its centre. You have only to recall those sickening moments of vertigo, or read about people suffering from inner ear imbalances or the catastrophic loss of their sense of position, to realise how casually, how vitally, the gyroscope of zero holds each of our voyaging reference-frames on course.

Is there, like the dot within the circle of one of the zeroes we came across (that theca or theta), a different zero in the mind from the zero of the body that carries it about? Nothing like a balance – closer, perhaps, to the centre of Pascal's infinite sphere, which is everywhere: since each of us correctly knows that ours is the unique centre. We call it 'I', and suppose that others, in some way that imagination alone can grasp, mean by it for their selves what we mean by it for ours. Recognising that they say 'I' in the same way we do severs at the same time that it connects us definitively to the world.

It is a paradox we accommodate ourselves to without ever resolving. So a singer brought up to practise the scales with C always taken as 'doh' is disconcerted to learn that in another tradition 'doh' names the first note of whatever key a piece is in. To protest that nevertheless 'doh' is really C and that 'I' rightly belongs only to me is to run foul of the movable 'doh' and the indiscriminate use of the personal pronoun. We may never manage to do more than translate these alien usages into our proper, solipsistic, tongue.

And this zero of self – since it lies behind sense, do we grasp it as absence? If it is the grasper, do we grasp it at all? Perhaps in stalled moments; perhaps as a flicker out the corner of the eye; perhaps as a shadow in the slanting light of fear, never coming on a snake

> Without a tighter breathing
> And zero at the bone.

Danger makes us know that we store something precious – but not what it is. We bear a message we cannot read, like those Greek runners who carried the long thin ribbons that had been written on when they were wound around a staff, and whose words would only make sense when the letter halves came together again on the matching staff of the receiver.

opposite:
Big Nothing
Margarita Gluzberg
1999

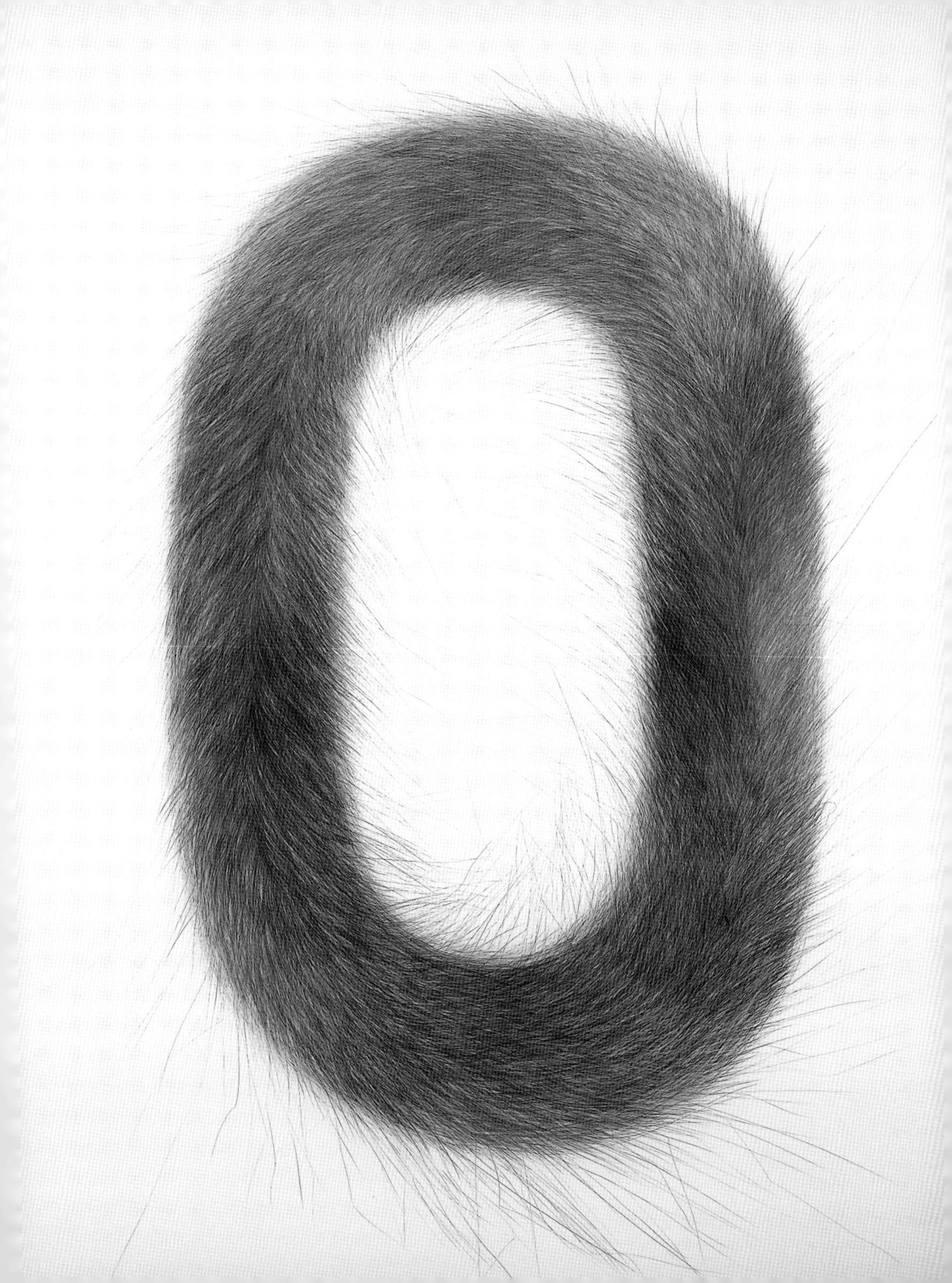

The Book of Sand
Jorge Luis Borges

Thy rope of sands...
George Herbert (1593–1623)

The line consists of an infinite number of points; the plane, of an infinite number of lines; the volume, of an infinite number of planes; the hypervolume, of an infinite number of volumes... No – this, *more geometrico*, is decidedly not the best way to begin my tale. To say that the story is true is by now a convention of every fantastic tale; mine, nevertheless, *is* true.

I live alone, in a fifth-floor apartment on Calle Belgrano. One evening a few months ago, I heard a knock at my door. I opened it, and a stranger stepped in. He was a tall man, with blurred, vague features, or perhaps my nearsightedness made me see him that way. Everything about him spoke of honest poverty: he was dressed in grey, and carried a grey valise. I immediately sensed that he was a foreigner. At first I thought he was old; then I noticed that I had been misled by his sparse hair, which was blonde, almost white, like the Scandinavians'. In the course of our conversation, which I doubt lasted more than an hour, I learned that he hailed from the Orkneys.

I pointed the man to a chair. He took some time to begin talking. He gave off an air of melancholy, as I myself do now.

'I sell Bibles,' he said at last.

'In this house,' I replied, not without a somewhat stiff, pedantic note, 'there are several English Bibles, including the first one, Wyclif's. I also have Cipriano de Valera's, Luther's (which is, in literary terms, the worst of the lot), and a Latin copy of the Vulgate. As you see, it isn't exactly Bibles I might be needing.'

After a brief silence he replied.

'It's not only Bibles I sell. I can show you a sacred book that might interest a man such as yourself. I came by it in northern India, in Bikaner.'

He opened his valise and brought out the book. He laid it on the table. It was a clothbound octavo volume, that had clearly passed through many hands. I examined it; the unusual heft of it surprised me. On the spine was printed *Holy Writ*, and then *Bombay*.

'Nineteenth-century, I'd say,' I observed.

'I don't know,' was the reply. 'Never did know.'

I opened it at random. The characters were unfamiliar to me. The pages, which seemed worn and badly set, were printed in double columns, like a Bible. The text was cramped, composed into versicles. At the upper corner of each page were Arabic numerals. I was struck by an odd fact: the even-numbered page would carry the number 40,514, let us say, while the odd-numbered page that followed it would be 999. I turned the page; the next page bore an eight-digit number. It also bore a small illustration, like those ones sees in dictionaries: an anchor drawn in pen and ink, as though by the unskilled hand of a child.

It was at that point that the stranger spoke again.

'Look at it well. You will never see it again.'

There was a threat in the words, but not in the voice.

I took note of the page, and then closed the book. Immediately I opened it again. In vain I searched for the figure of the anchor, page after page. To hide my discomforture, I tried another tack.

'This is a version of the Scripture in some Hindu language, isn't that right?'

'No,' he replied.

Then he lowered his voice, as though entrusting me with a secret.

'I came across this book in a village on the plain, and I traded a few rupees and a Bible for it. The man who owned it didn't know how to read. I suspect he saw the Book of Books as an amulet. He was of the lowest caste; people could not so much as step on his shadow without being defiled. He told me his book was called the Book of Sand because neither sand nor this has a beginning or an end.'

He suggested I try to find the first page.

I took the cover in my left hand and opened the book, my thumb and forefinger almost touching. It was impossible: several pages always lay between the cover and my hand. It was as though they grew from the very book.

'Now try to find the end.'

I failed there as well.

'This can't be,' I stammered, my voice hardly recognisable as my own.

'It can't be, yet it *is*,' the Bible peddler said, his voice little more than a whisper. 'The number of pages in this book is literally infinite. No page is the first page; no page is the last. I don't know why they're numbered in this arbitrary way, but perhaps it's to give one to understand that the terms of an infinite series can be numbered any way whatever.'

Then, as though thinking out loud, he went on.

'If space is infinite, we are anywhere, at any point in space. If time is infinite, we are at any point in time.'

His musing irritated me.

'You,' I said, 'are a religious man, are you not?'

'Yes, I'm Presbyterian. My conscience is clear. I am certain I didn't cheat that native when I gave him the Lord's Word in exchange for his diabolic book.'

I assured him he had nothing to reproach himself for, and asked whether he was just passing through the country. He replied that he planned to return to his own country within a few days. It was then that I learned he was a Scot and that his home was in the Orkneys. I told him I had great personal fondness for Scotland because of my love for Stevenson and Hume.

'And Robbie Burns,' he corrected.

As we talked I continued to explore the infinite book.

'Had you intended to offer this curious specimen to the British Museum then?' I asked with feigned indifference.

'No,' he replied, 'I am offering it to you,' and he mentioned a great sum of money.

I told him, with perfect honesty, that such an amount of money was not within my ability to pay. But my mind was working; in a few moments I had devised my plan.

'I propose a trade,' I said. 'You purchased the volume with a few rupees and the Holy Scripture; I will offer you the full sum of my pension, which I have just received, and Wyclif's black-letter Bible. It was left to me by my parents.'

'A black-letter Wyclif!' he murmured.

I went to my bedroom and brought back the money and the book.

With a bibliophile's zeal he turned the pages and studied the binding.

'Done,' he said.

I was astonished that he did not haggle. Only later was I to realise that he had entered my house already determined to sell the book. He did not count the money, but merely put the bills into his pocket.

We chatted about India, the Orkneys, and the Norwegian jarls that had once ruled those islands. Night was falling when the man left. I have never seen him since, nor do I know his name.

I thought of putting the Book of Sand in the space left by the Wyclif, but I chose at last to hide it behind some imperfect volumes of *The Thousand and One Nights*.

I went to bed but could not sleep. At three or four in the morning I turned on the light. I took out the impossible book and turned its pages. On one, I saw an engraving of a mask. There was a number in the corner of the page – I don't remember now what it was – raised to the ninth power.

I showed no-one my treasure. To the joy of possession was added the fear that it would be stolen from me, and to that, the suspicion that it might not be truly infinite. Those two points of anxiety aggravated my already habitual misanthropy. I had but a few friends left, and those, I stopped seeing. A prisoner of the Book, I hardly left my house. I examined the worn binding and the covers with a magnifying glass, and rejected the possibility of some artifice. I found that the small illustrations were spaced at two-thousand-page intervals. I began noting them down in an alphabetical notebook, which was very soon filled. They never repeated themselves. At night, during the rare intervals spared me by insomnia, I dreamed of the book.

Summer was drawing to a close, and I realised that the book was monstrous. It was cold consolation to think that I, who looked upon it with my eyes and fondled it with my ten flesh-and-bone fingers, was no less monstrous than the book. I felt it was a nightmare thing, an obscene thing, and that it defiled and corrupted reality.

I considered fire, but I feared that the burning of an infinite book might be similarly infinite, and suffocate the planet in smoke.

I remembered reading once that the best place to hide a leaf is in the forest. Before my retirement I had worked in the National Library, which contained nine hundred thousand books; I knew that to the right of the lobby a curving staircase descended into the shadows of the basement, where the maps and periodicals are kept. I took advantage of the librarians' distraction to hide the Book of Sand on one of the library's damp shelves; I tried not to notice how high up, or how far from the door.

I now feel a little better, but I refuse to even walk down the street the library's on.

The Long Winter of Mars
Joe Woodhouse
2000

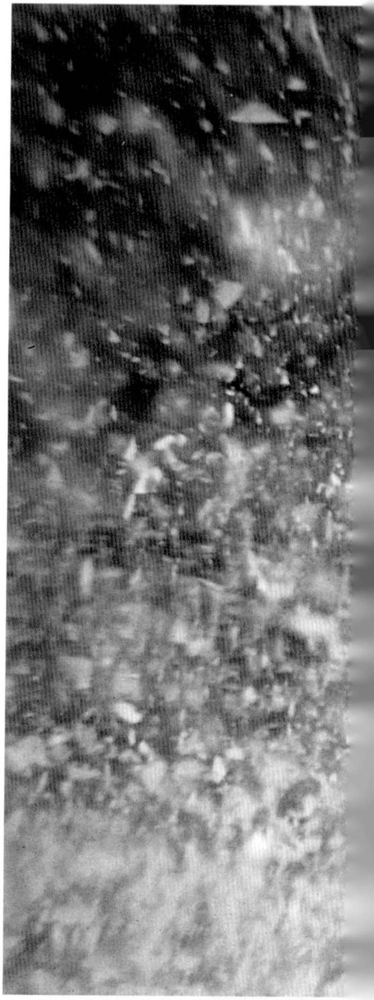

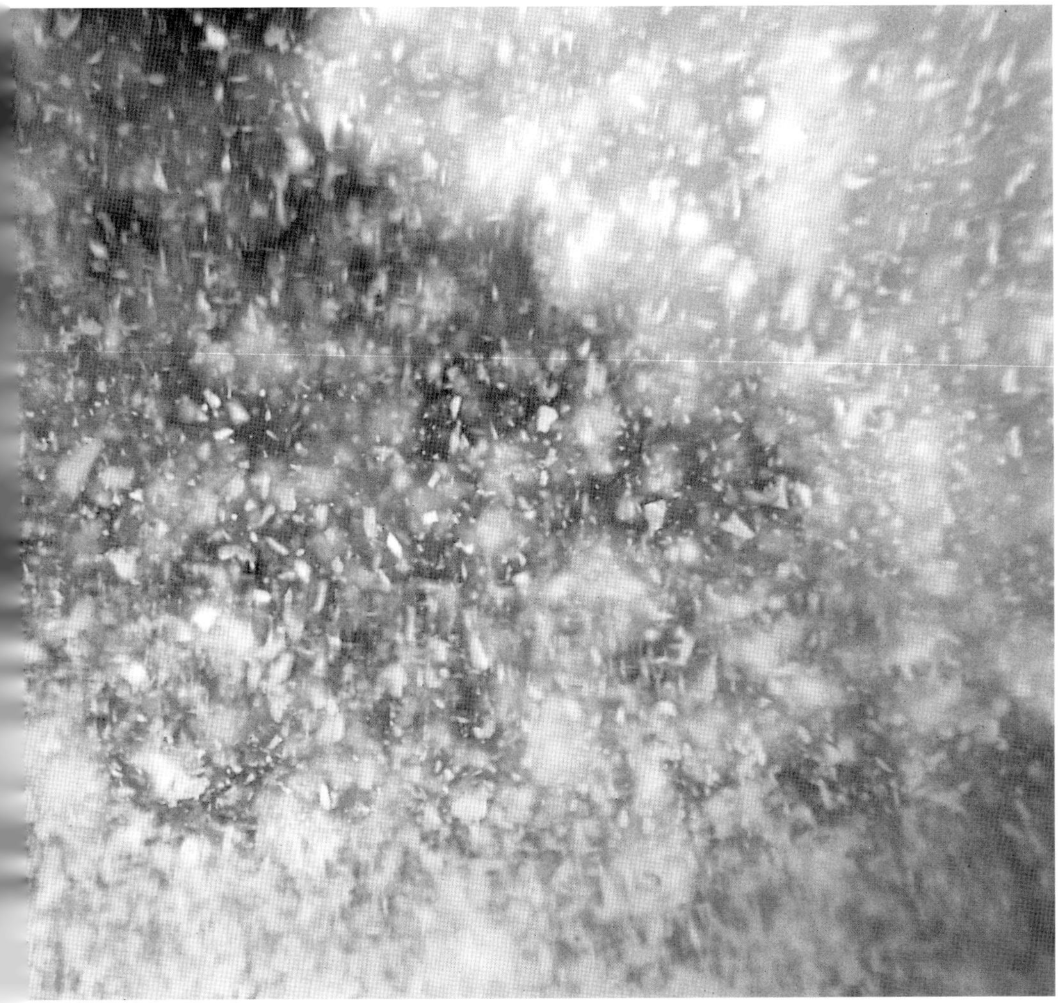

Book of Dust
Agnes Denes

Dust is particulate matter, the dispersed, disordered raw material from which everything ordered and coherent arises, and it is to dust that the complex decays.

From the beginning to the end, dust underlies all existence. It is the species of light one sees flickering in a sunbeam, the molecules of gas dashing randomly in all directions. It is the atoms and molecules of matter that can be recombined and reshaped into something new such as the ordered array of atoms in a crystal or in a living cell, and it is the dusts of interstellar space that condensed to produce the sun and its planets and all the galaxies.

Everything that we understand as consistent, the living creature, the machine, the tree, are dust in its coherent phase, part of its continuous evolutionary cycle from order to disorder, from growth to decay repeated in seemingly endless variations.

According to the second law of thermodynamics, entropy is forever increasing in the universe, and with it the chaotic phase of dust, destined to triumph over order. Nonetheless, we see order arising out of chaos everywhere as the random dust of earth are assembled into complex living things. This apparent negative entropy allows us to question if life has a quality that supersedes the laws of physics and negates the claims that this order is forever and irreversibly increasing. Life, however, is an integral part of the universe, and cannot be isolated from it. The price of organisation is increased entropy everywhere, even if it is deferred or invisible.

Life is powered by a sun that has lived millions of times longer than the humans and the cycles we see are tiny ripples in a system that takes billions of years to run down. These cycles are open ended. Every time a thing is born and later dies and decays, the world does not return to where it was before the cycle. The dust to which decay returns is greater than the dust that had created it. The cycles of life and death increase entropy; with each revolution the net disorder increases in the universe. The disordered phase in the nature of dust grows at the expense of its ordered one.

Even the lives of stars seem cyclic. Our sun contains the debris of older generations of stars, and this cosmic recycling may last forever. But even the life of a star is only a moment in the total life of our universe, and the birth and death of generations of stars increase disorder just as life does, and there will eventually be a final generation of stars after which there will be no more.

Pockets of dusts becoming organised and cycling through death and rejuvenation are local phenomena; pulsations immersed in a background of disorder and are doomed to die out eventually.

Even the universe may not be exempt from this principle. If the whole universe ultimately collapses and then rebounds to start over again, the next cycle will not be as energetic as this one was. The entropy and disorder that are being produced in this universe are so fundamental that they are likely to survive the death of the universe and effect the next cycle.

The dusts of our universe are more than raw material being transformed back and forth between consistency and disarray. Within themselves they contain many levels of both organisation and chaos. The nucleus of an atom can be located with high precision, but the electrons that create its envelope are in elusive disarray. The atoms are positioned precisely in molecules and arrange themselves in perfect arrays called crystals. Most solid matter is crystalline, but consists of disordered microcrystals. Most dust particles have crystalline interiors, but the microcrystal in one speck of dust cannot coordinate its order with that of another grain, and the dust remains chaotic. Yet it is from these dusts that the complexities of our civilisation are built. Dust on one level is chaotic, and orderly and precise on another.

As the universe evolves it creates new dusts for its various eras. At the beginning the dust of the universe was most likely high energy packed radiation. This soon decayed into a hot, compressed soup of quarks, which in turn condensed into the ordinary nuclei and matter of our present universe. Eventually all matter is likely to decay, and the only dusts larger than an electron will be black holes more massive than our sun. But even black holes decay, and if the universe lasts long enough the ultimate dust will be greatly diluted cold radiation in a vast vacuum.

The dusts of our era, though but a transitory formation in an evolving universe, will persist for many trillions of years. Its great miracle, life, is a cycle of ordered dust that strives to perpetuate itself. The great by-product of life, intelligence, is also like dust, with bits and fragments of coherence being produced out of disorder, but all too often lapses back into chaos again.

The transformation of dust into life and intelligence can survive as long as there is organisable matter in the universe, and as long as there is matter there will be energy to power this transformation. These isolated pockets of order called life could survive for countless trillions of years in a universe forever decaying. Finally the greatest product of order, intelligence, becomes a factor in our universe that may one day challenge its most fundamental law – that disorder is the ultimate fate of all.

That ultimate anthropocentric view that we are the centre of the universe is true in a sense. In this universe of extremes humanity is almost in the centre of its range of sizes, masses and temperatures. We are macroscopic, in the middle between cosmic and microscopic proportions. Our size is the geometric mean between atoms and the stars, 10 billion times larger than an atom, 10 billion times smaller than the sun. We are the mean between the ultra microscopic (quarks and Planck length), and the whole visible universe. Our world begins at the surface of our skin and we can peer inward and out to equal depths. Similarly, our body temperature, 300 K, is the geometric mean between the 3 K temperature of the universe and the 30,000 K temperature of the hottest stars. Even our earth is a medium planet: there are four smaller and four larger in the solar system. We occupy a thin layer on the surface of the earth between its molten interior and frigid outer space.

Midway between these extremes of large and small numbers, in a hostile universe, we have found our narrow niche with a body large enough to develop the complicated mechanisms needed to generate intelligence, yet small enough not to be crushed by our own weight: at a temperature in which the molecules of our bodies simultaneously have the stability associated with low temperatures

OUR UNIVERSE

Age:	7–20 billion yrs (100–300 million human lifetimes)
Size:	7–20 billion light years, visible universe (v.u.)
Life span:	100 billion yrs minimum – possibly infinite
Mass:	10^{56} g – for visible universe
Composition:	hydrogen 75%, helium 23%, other elements 2%

	MICROSCOPIC	**HUMAN SCALE**	**COSMIC**
Size	10^{-33} cm (Planck length)	200 cm (person)	10^{28} cm (universe)
Velocity	10^{-7} cm/sec (continental drift)	100 cm/sec (man walking)	3 x 10^{10} cm/sec (velocity of light)
Power	10^{-9} watts (neuron in brain)	10 – 20 watts (human heart)	4 x 10^{26} watts (sun)
Numbers	less than 10 (kinds of stable particles)	10^{30} (atoms in human)	10^{80} (atoms in universe)
Density	10^{-16} gm/cm3 (nucleus)	1 gm/cm^3 (human)	5 x 10^{-30} gm/cm3 (universe)
Mass	10^{-28} g (electron)	10^5 g (human)	10^{45} gm (galaxy)
Temperature	3 K (cosmic background radiation)	310 K (human body temperature)	10^7 K (centre of sun)

and the versatility for intricate reactions and complex chemistry without destroying themselves as they would at higher temperatures. The largest thing we know is the universe itself, 10^{28} cm, while the smallest is the Planck Length, the fundamental unit of quantum gravity, 10^{-33} cm. The geometric mean between the two, $\sqrt{10^{28} \text{ x } 10^{-33}}$ - 0.003 cm, is the size of the average living cell, practically the size of man compared to the extremes that exist in the universe. Therefore life itself seems to be in the middle of existence, equidistant between two extremes.

Could our position in the centre of things be a selection effect, the consequence of our ability to measure things, or even to comprehend them? Perhaps the degree of our ability to measure the microscopic equals the extent to which we can measure the cosmic or megascopic, and we are in truth the geometric mean of the capacity of our measuring tools, placing us in a false centre of things. In that case we would believe ourselves to be in the centre of the universe no matter what our magnitude, and everywhere in the universe there must be a kind of anthropocentricity existing where everything perceives itself as the centre from a microbe to a galaxy to a universe to a god.

extracted from *The Book of Dust – The Beginning and the End of Time and Thereafter*

opposite:
Gap Fillers
Carey Young
2001

overleaf:
Lecture on Nothing
(excerpt)
John Cage
1959

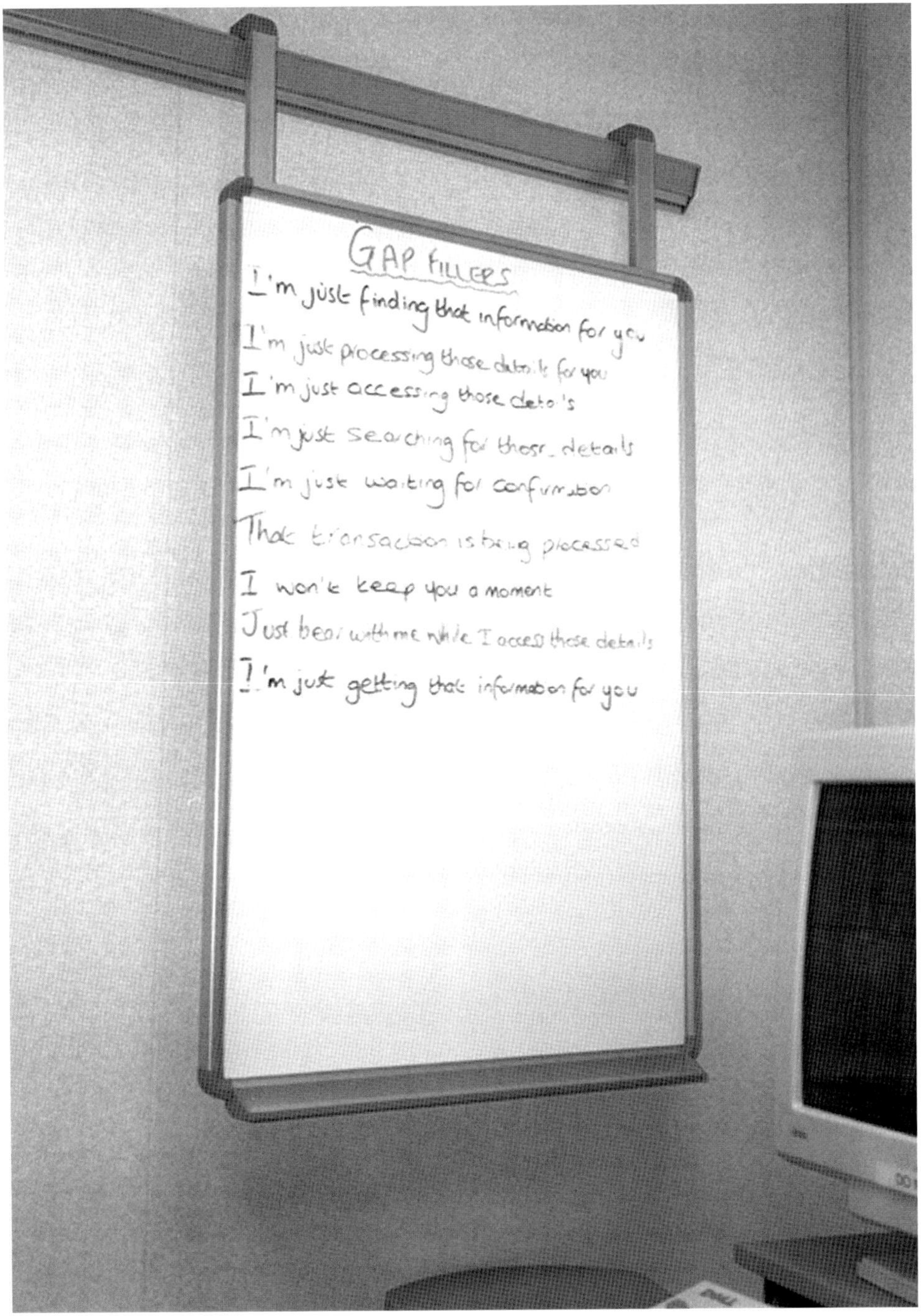
GAP FILLERS
I'm just finding that information for you
I'm just processing those details for you
I'm just accessing those details
I'm just searching for those details
I'm just waiting for confirmation
That transaction is being processed
I won't keep you a moment
Just bear with me while I access those details
I'm just getting that information for you

This lecture was printed in Incontri Musicali, *August 1959. There are four measures in each line and twelve lines in each unit of the rhythmic structure. There are forty-eight such units, each having forty-eight measures. The whole is divided into five large parts, in the proportion 7, 6, 14, 14, 7. The forty-eight measures of each unit are likewise so divided. The text is printed in four columns to facilitate a rhythmic reading. Each line is to be read across the page from left to right, not down the columns in sequence. This should not be done in an artificial manner (which might result from an attempt to be too strictly faithful to the position of the words on the page), but with the* rubato *which one uses in everyday speech.*

LECTURE ON NOTHING

I am here , and there is nothing to say .
If among you are
those who wish to get somewhere , let them leave at
any moment . What we re–quire is
silence ; but what silence requires
is that I go on talking .
Give any one thought
a push : it falls down easily
; but the pusher and the pushed pro–duce that enter–
tainment called a dis–cussion .
Shall we have one later ?

♍

Or , we could simply de–cide not to have a dis–
cussion . What ever you like . But
now there are silences and the
words make help make the
silences .

I have nothing to say
and I am saying it and that is
poetry as I need it .

This space of time is organized
. We need not fear these silences, —
♍

we may love them .
This is a composed
talk , for I am making it
just as I make a piece of music. It is like a glass
of milk . We need the glass
and we need the milk . Or again it is like an
empty glass into which at any
moment anything may be poured
. As we go along , (who knows?)
an i–dea may occur in this talk .
I have no idea whether one will
or not. If one does, let it. Re–

♍

gard it as something seen momentarily , as
though from a window while traveling .
If across Kansas , then, of course, Kansas
. Arizona is more interesting,
almost too interesting , especially for a New–Yorker who is
being interested in spite of himself in everything. Now he knows he
needs the Kansas in him . Kansas is like
nothing on earth , and for a New Yorker very refreshing.
It is like an empty glass , nothing but wheat , or
is it corn ? Does it matter which ?
Kansas has this about it: at any instant, one may leave it,
and whenever one wishes one may return to it .

♍

Or you may leave it forever and never return to it ,
for we pos–sess nothing . Our poetry now
is the reali–zation that we possess nothing
. Anything therefore is a delight
(since we do not pos–sess it) and thus need not fear its loss
. We need not destroy the past: it is gone;
at any moment, it might reappear and seem to be and be the present
. Would it be a repetition? Only if we thought we
owned it, but since we don't, it is free and so are we

Let us then see what we are thinking about when we speak of "Nothing." To represent "Nothing," we must either imagine it or conceive it. Let us examine what this image or this idea may be. First, the image.

I am going to close my eyes, stop my ears, extinguish one by one the sensations that come to me from the outer world. Now it is done; all my perceptions vanish, the material universe sinks into silence and the night.—I subsist, however, and cannot help myself subsisting. I am still there, with the organic sensations which come to me from the surface and from the interior of my body, with the recollections which my past perceptions have left behind them—nay, with the impression, most positive and full, of the void I have just made about me. How can I suppress all this? How eliminate myself? I can even, it may be, blot out and forget my recollections up to my immediate past; but at least I keep the consciousness of my present reduced to its extremest poverty, that is to say, of the actual state of my body. I will try, however, to do away even with this consciousness itself. I will reduce more and more the sensations my body sends in to me: now they are almost gone; now they are gone, they have disappeared in the night where all things else have already died away. But no! At the very instant that my consciousness is extinguished, another consciousness lights up—or rather, it was already alight: it had arisen the instant before, in order to witness the extinction of the first; for the first could disappear only for another and in the presence of another. I see myself annihilated only if I have already resuscitated myself by an act which is positive, however involuntary and unconscious. So, do what I will, I am always perceiving something, either from without or from within. When I no longer know anything of external objects, it is because I have taken refuge in

margin notes on
Creative Evolution
Sarah Dobai

Bergson's sensibility seems to be drawn to death – the inorganic – the scene without a self –

the consciousness that I have of myself. If I abolish this inner self, its very abolition becomes an object for an imaginary self which now perceives as an external object the self that is dying away. Be it external or internal, some object there always is that my imagination is representing. My imagination, it is true, can go from one to the other, I can by turns imagine a nought of external perception or a nought of internal perception, but not both at once, for the absence of one consists, at bottom, in the exclusive presence of the other. But, from the fact that two relative noughts are imaginable in turn, we wrongly conclude that they are imaginable together: a conclusion the absurdity of which must be obvious, for we cannot imagine a nought without perceiving, at least confusedly, that we are imagining it, consequently that we are acting, that we are thinking, and therefore that something still subsists.

The image, then, properly so called, of a suppression of everything is never formed by thought. The effort by which we strive to create this image simply ends in making us swing to and fro between the vision of an outer and that of an inner reality. In this coming and going of our mind between the without and the within, there is a point, at equal distance from both, in which it seems to us that we no longer perceive the one, and that we do not yet perceive the other: it is there that the image of "Nothing" is formed. In reality, we then perceive both, having reached the point where the two terms come together, and the image of Nothing, so defined, is an image full of things, an image that includes at once that of the subject and that of the object and, besides, a perpetual leaping from one to the other and the refusal ever to come to rest finally on either. Evidently this is not the nothing that we can oppose to being, and put before or be-

until "It follows from this double analysis that the idea of absolute nought, in the sense of the annihilation of everything, is a self-destructive idea, a pseudo idea, a mere word."

from p 283. "the representation of the void is always a representation which is full and which resolves itself on analysis into two positive elements, the idea of a substitution and the feeling experienced or imagined of a desire or regret"

A PLACE WHERE NOTHING HAS HAPPENED

The Place was a piece of land and a few derelict buildings in Newcastle, between the riverfront and the railway line. In the late 1980s, it had been earmarked for redevelopment but, as the necessary money was never forthcoming, by 1993, the area was still a site-in-waiting. The Place had developed a transitory half-life: people occupied the empty buildings and fixed cars on the waste ground; there were traces of all sorts of activity, some of which were obviously illegal.

I requested that a Scenes of Crime Officer from Northumbria Police consider the Place as a crime scene where the crime was unspecified. He spent an afternoon photographing and taking samples from a cordoned-off section of the site. The samples he took broke down into roughly three areas:

SAMPLES WHICH IDENTIFY THE SITE AS UNIQUE
These were small pieces of glass, brickwork, soil, etc. the likes of which would be unwittingly removed from the site on clothing and footwear by anyone who had spent time there. These samples were of the type that would be put in storage so that when articles were available from a detained suspect, a comparative analysis could be made.

SAMPLES WHICH ARE VISIBLE INDICATIONS OF HUMAN ACTIVITY
These were comprised mostly of casts: either in plaster for footprints and tyre tracks; or in rubber dental mould material (for more detail) for traces of tool marks which indicate forced entry. Distinctive marks left on dust-covered objects were lifted on clear, sticky-backed plastic – for example, trouser creases from someone who had been kneeling. As with the first sample, these traces were of the type that could be retained for comparison in forensic analysis.

SAMPLES WHICH ARE INVISIBLE INDICATIONS OF HUMAN ACTIVITY
These were objects (mostly discarded rubbish) which are likely to retain clear fingerprints: for example, wrappers and aluminium cans. Fingerprinting was also done on-site and the prints lifted and retained on clear, sticky-backed plastic.

The labelled objects, laid out on glass tables and accompanied by the police officer's notes, were displayed in a portakabin placed relatively discreetly on the site. Black-and-white photos were pinned to the walls. The portakabin became an incident room for a non-specific incident, providing an accurate record of the area for a unique moment in time.

Christine Borland, 1993

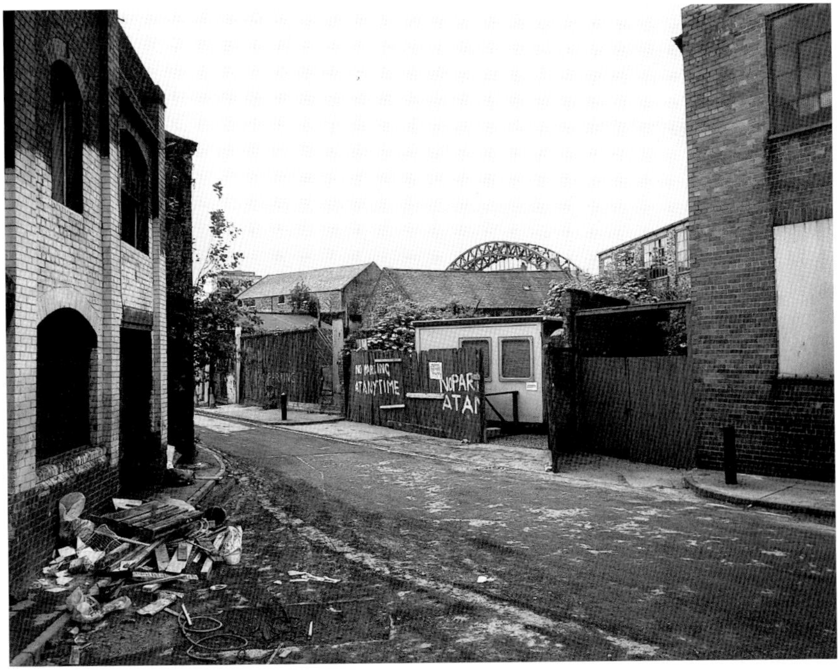
ATANYTIME

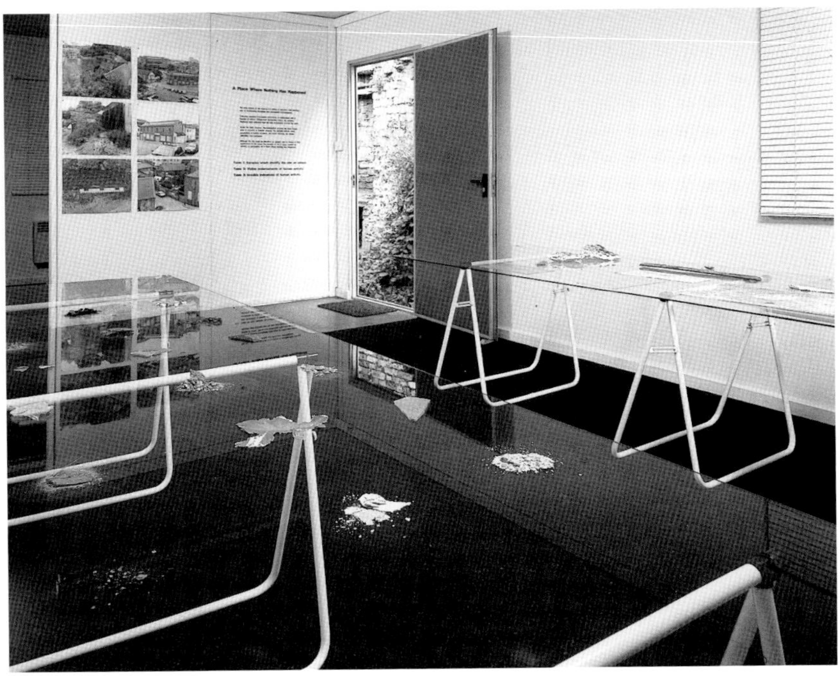

everythingispossibleexceptthatwhichis

deemedimpossiblebythenatureofthings

from the california civil code

ELLIS UNIT 1 HUNTSVILLE TEXAS

COMMISSARY PRICE LIST

POWDERED DRINKS

JFG Cool Off	.08
Tea Bags	.03

FRUIT DRINKS

Grapefruit	.30
Orange	.30
Pineapple	.30
V-8	.30
Tomato	.23
Pineapple - Grapefruit	.25

CANNED DRINKS

Big Red	.33
Coca Cola	.33
Diet Dr. Pepper	.33
Diet Sprite	.33
Dr. Pepper	.33
Minute Maid Orange	.33
Root Beer	.33
Sprite	.33
Diet Coke	.33
Cream Soda	.22
Strawberry	.22

COCOA & HOT CHOCOLATE

Hershey's Syrup	.55
Hot Chocolate (Bag)	1.75
Hot Chocolate (Ind.)	.10

CANNED & POWDERED MILK

Canned Milk	.30
Ensure	.55
Alba Nonfat Dry Milk	.40
Sugar Substitute	1.65

COFFEE

Decaff. Coffee	.10
JFG	1.60
JFG Decaff.	2.25
JFG Freeze Dried	5.50
Maryland Club	2.50
Maxwell House	2.25
Taster's Choice	2.80
Nescafe	2.25

DAIRY PRODUCTS

Gouda Cheese (Sliced)	.15
Philadelphia Cream Cheese	.15
Snack Cheese	1.25
Oleo	.16

ICE CREAM

Blue Bell	3.50
Blue Bell	1.00
Bombstick	.25
Fudge-sicle	.15
Cookies 'N Cream Sandwich	.19
Eskimo Pie	.25
Grizzly Bar	.15
Mellorine	1.40
Neopolitan Sandwich	.25
Nestle Crunch	.25
Nuts-to-You	.22
Yogart	1.30

MISCELLANEOUS SEAFOOD

Mackerel	.80
Salmon	1.35
Sardines	.50
Tuna	.85

CANNED MEATS

Beans & Weiners	.60
Beef Stew	.65
Canned Luncheon Meat	1.75
Chicken Vienna	.40
Chicken & Dumplings	.40
Chili Con Carne	.65
Chili	.75
Chunky Chicken	1.10
Chunky Ham	1.25
Chunky Turkey	1.10
Corned Beef	.50
Deviled Spam	.50
Lasagna	.40
Noodles & Chicken	.40
Potted Meat	.35
Roast Beef W/Gravy	1.80
Shells and Sausage	.45
Sloppy Joes	1.10
Spaghetti & Beef	.45
Tamales	.75
Vienna Sausage	.60

CONDIMENTS

Bean Dip	.75
Mandarin Oranges	.50
Mexican Beans	.45
Pork & Beans	.40
Potato Sticks	.25
Refried Beans	.45
Salt, Mini	.10
Salt Substitute	.95

DRY SOUP MIX

Bouillon Cubes	.25
Ramen Noodles	.25

PICKLES, PEPPERS, ONIONS

Jalapeno Peppers	.20
Kosher Pickles	.35
P.C. Onions	.04

CATSUP, BBQ SAUCE, SAUCES

BBQ Sauce	.75
Ketchup, Hunt's	1.00
Picante Sauce	.90
Louisiana Hot Sauce	.35

JELLIES & PEANUT BUTTER

Grape Jelly, Crystal	.90
Peanut Butter	1.50
Srawberry Preserves	1.25

DRESSINGS & MUSTARD

Mustard	.60
Salad Dressing	.90
Sandwich Spread	.90

CHIPS, SNACKS & CRACKERS

Cheese Popcorn	.15
Cheetos	.25
Cheez-Its	.15
Cheddar Cheese Nips	1.25
Dorito	.25
Fritos	.25
Potato Chips	.25
Hot Fries	.17
Tostitoes	1.40
R & R Tortilla Chips	1.40
Saltine Crackers	.20
Snack Crackers	.80
Super Snacks	1.05
Austin PNB Crackers	.15

COOKIES

Almost Home Cookies	1.25
Jackson Cookies	.75
Keebler ELFudge Cookies	1.25
Rip-On Cookies	(as priced)
Striped Shortbread, Nab.	.65
Vanilla Wafers	.60
Moon Pies	.25

CANDY

Candy	.30 & .35
Mint Sticks	.10
One Cent Candy	.01
Pay Day	.25
Peanut Patty	.30
Slo-Poke	.08
Tootsie Pops	.08
Two Cent Candy	.02

BAG CANDY

Butterscotch	.70
Jolly Rancher Kisses	.45
Lemon Drops	.70
Orange Slices	.70

BREAD & PASTRIES

White Bread	.75
Wheat Bread	as priced
Small Pastries	.35
Tortillas	as priced

INSTANT BREAKFAST

Kudo Bar	.30
Oatmeal, Instant	.20
Toastettes	.90

CELLO NUTS

Honey Roasted Cashews	.85
Honey Roasted Peanuts	.50
Spanish Peanuts	.75

CIGARETTES

No Name	1.00
Dorals	1.00
Regular	1.30
Richland	.95

SNUFF

Copenhagen	1.65
Hawken	1.25
Honest	2.85
Kodiak	1.25
Skoal	1.65
Snuff, Bottle	2.85
Snuff, Sweet	3.40
Snuff, Can	.40
Tube Rose	1.00

PIPE TOBACCO

Argosy Black	1.45
Borkum Riff	1.45
Cherry Blend	1.05
Half & Half	.85
Prince Albert	.95
Rum & Maple	1.05
Sir Walter Raleigh (ARO)	1.05
Sir Walter Raleigh (Pouch)	.85

CHEWING TOBACCO

Beechnut	1.10
Bull Of The Woods	1.00
Cannonball	1.00
Day's Work	1.10
Levi Garret	1.25
Levi Garret Plug	1.00
R J Gold	1.00
Red Man	1.25
Red Man Plug	1.10

CIGARS

Dixie Maid	.11
Don Cesar	.45
El Producto	.30
Havatampa	.17
King Edward	.15
King Edward Tips	.12
Roi Tan	.20
Swisher Sweets	15
Swisher Sweets Tips	.12

CIGARETTE TOBACCO

Canned Bugler	3.60
Bugler, Package	.55
Canned Kite	4.45
Kite, Package	.60
Our Advertiser	.30

SMOKING ACCESSORIES

Cigarette Case	.60
Cigarette Roller	1.25
Cigarette Roller Rep. S	.35
Matches	.04
Pipe Cleaners	.40
Pipe Filters	.30
Pipes	3.25
Top Papers	.30

DENTAL HYGIENE

Colgate	1.05
Denquel	1.85
Dental Flossers	1.00
Denture Brush	.60
Efferdent	1.85
Fasteeth	2.25
Kleenite	1.90
Listerine	.60
Oral B Toothpaste	.65
Poligrip	1.25
Sensodyne Toothpaste	2.35
Toothbrushes	.35
Toothbrush Holders	.50
Ultra Brite	.95
Vi-Jon Mouthwash	.95
Landers Mouthwash	.90

SHAVING

Afta, Mennen	1.90
Brushless Shave	1.10
Bumphree	2.85
Dispos. Shavers	.15
EF Kay Shaving Cream	1.50
EF Kay Shaving Gel	1.50
Magic After Shave Lotion	1.55
Magic Shave Cream Tube	1.70
Razor Head / HP 1622	10.25
Shave Mirror	4.95
Shave Brush	3.00
Shave Soap, Colgate	.60
Styptic Pencil	.50
Triple Razor Head	12.25

PRICES SUBJECT TO CHANGE WITHOUT NOTICE

S0870/p1

COMMISSARY PRICE LIST

PRICES SUBJECT TO CHANGE WITHOUT NOTICE ...

SOAPS

A[illegible] Cocoa Butter Soap	1.00
An[illegible] Complexion Bar	1.00
Dial Soap	.40
Irish Spring	.40
Jergens Soap	.40

CREAMS & LOTIONS

Ambi Cocoa Butter Cream	2.00
Ambi Skin Tone Cream	2.75
Ashway Skin Lotion	1.70
Cocoa Butter Lotion, Ba	1.95
Jergens	1.90
Lander's Aloe Vera Cream	.50
Lander's Cocoa Butter, L	.50
Lander's Cocoa Butter, C	.50
Lander's Collagen Cream	.50
Lander's Honey & Almond	.50
Lander's Medicated Cream	.50
Lubriderm Lotion	1.85
Prime Vit. E Cream	1.95

GROOMING SUPPLIES

Baby Lotion, Baby Magic	1.25
Baby Oil, Baby Magic	1.40
Baby Powder, Baby Magic	1.40
Bath Talc	1.85
Dial Roll-On	1.35
Emery Boards	.40
English Leather Cologne	3.50
English Leather Hand Lo.	1.35
Lander's Roll-On Deodor	.95
Nail Clippers	.45
Q'Tips	.95
Quinsana Plus, Foot Pow.	2.25
Speed Stick	1.75

HAIR CARE

Baby Shampoo, Baby Magic	1.50
Glo-Sheen	1.20
Hair Brush, Men's	1.00
Lander's Balsam Condit.	.50
Lander's Black Orchid H.	.50
Lander's Dandruff Shamp.	.50
Lander's Herbal Shampoo	.50
Lander's Hair Gel	.95
M-S Hair Food, United L	1.05
M-S Lanolin Conditioner	1.05
M-S Sulphur Plus, Unite.	1.05
Magnificent Hair Food	1.40
Pocket Combs	.10
Posner Easy Wave	1.40
Protein 21	1.25
Protein 29	1.50
QED Hair Cream	1.25
Royal Crown	.65
Selsun Blue	.45
Vitamin E Shampoo	1.95
Baby Shampoo, Lander's	1.25
Blue Mag. Bergamot	1.30
Blue Mag. Cholesterol H.	1.70
Sulphur 8	1.75

MISC HBA

Acne	3.30
Alka Seltzer	.25
Blistex Lip Balm	.50
Certs	.25
Chap-et Lip Kote	.50
Luden's Cough Drops	.75
Petroleum Jelly	1.25
Saltine Solution, Contact	2.35
Skintona	1.90
Tums	.30

VITAMINS

Maxi-Vitamins	2.75
Protein Tablets	1.70
Vitamin C	1.50
Vitamin E	2.75
Vitamin Tablets w/Iron	1.70
Body Builder Powder	.40

ART SUPPLIES

Water Colors	1.00
Drawing Pad	2.00
Color Pencils	.95
Artist's Brushes	.50
Protractor	.25

WRITING MATERIALS

Carbon Paper	[illegible]
Dictionary	[illegible]
Dictionary, Spanish	[illegible]
Lead Pencils	.07
Legal Pads	[illegible]
Notebook Binders, Mead	[illegible]
Notebook Paper	[illegible]
Onion Skin Paper - 8 ½ x 14	.03
Pencil Sharpeners	[illegible]
Pocket Dictionary	1.05
Pocket Notebook	.25
Sherlite Envelopes-Mens	1.00
Sherlite Tablets-Mens	1.00
Stamps, .25	.25
Stamps, .03	.03
Stamped Envelopes	.30
Stick Pens (Black)	.20
Typewriter	155.00
Typewriter Eraser	.30
Typewriter XL1000, Corr.	3.00
Typewriter XL1500, Corr.	3.50
Typewriter Ribbon	1.95
Typewriter Ribbon, (Elect.)	5.50
Typing Paper	.90

Wireless Notebook, Comp.	.65
Writ Envelopes	.25
Writ Paper	.02

GREETING CARDS

Card	.25
Card	.35
Card	.50
Card	.70

ELECTRICAL

Adaptors	as priced
Alarm Clock	5.00
Archer FM Booster	24.95
Battery Bedside Alarm C.	7.90
Brandon Radio	24.50
Stinger	3.75
Dipoles	1.05
Earbuds	5.00
Extension Cord	10.95
Fan, Small (6-inch)	8.85
Fan, Rotator (9-inch)	18.00
Headphone Ext. Cable	3.15
Jumper Cable (30-inch)	1.05
Matching Transformers	.50
Calculator, Solar	6.95
Calculator, Classroom	19.75
Deluxe FM Booster (25-A)	31.15
Realistic AM/FM Radio	39.95

WATCHES

Casio Watch #F-10	7.10
Casio Watch-Mel #M-1230	34.35
Pulsar #FS005	26.00
Pulsar #JS042	26.25
Pulsar #PFA083	23.50
Pulsar #PFA091	23.50
Pulsar #PRQ002	26.25
Pulsar #PFA158	23.50
Timex #78317	22.35
Timex #78578	13.25
Watchband, M.G. Reg. #5	8.75
Watchband, M.S. Long #6	5.25
Watchband, M.S. Reg. #5	5.25
Watchband, Nylon	.50

BATTERIES

Alarm Clock Battery, TY	1.55
Battery, Type D-377	1.55
Battery, DL1620 - Casio	2.50
Battery, Type A (D-303)	2.20
Battery, Type AA	1.05
Battery, Type B (D-343B)	1.55
Battery, Type C (D-323)	1.55
Battery, Type D (D-301)(D-319)	1.75
Battery, Type D-384	.80
Battery, Type D-395	1.50
Battery, Type F (D-393)	1.55
Battery, Type H (D-386)	1.55
Battery, (D-371)	.75
Battery, Type J (D-357)	1.80
Battery, Type K (D-392)	1.55
Battery, Type L (D-391)	1.55
Battery, Type M (M-389)	1.55
Battery, Type S (D-362)	1.55
Battery, Type T (D-390)	1.55
Battery, Type V (D-396)	1.35
Battery, Type W (ER-399)	1.55
Battery, #394	1.50
Battery, #2015-Casio	2.50

CLOTHING

Athletic Supporter	2.25
Athletic T-Shirts	1.80
Gloves, Cloth	1.50
Gloves, Gripper	1.60
Gloves, Leather Palm	4.45
Gloves, Leather Riding	10.25
Gym Shorts	3.95
Hand Towels	1.40
Handkerchiefs	.40
Shorts	2.30
Shorts, Size 46	2.60
Sweat Pants	6.30
Sweat Shirts	6.25
Big Man T-Shirts	4.00
T-Shirts	2.35
Thermal Pants	3.75
Thermal Shirts	4.15
Wash Cloths	.35
Red Top Tube Socks	1.55

MISCELLANEOUS

Can Openers	.55
Combination Locks	4.50
Commissary Bags	1.80
Plastic Bowls	.30
Plastic Mugs	.40
Soap Dish	.30
Spoon, H.D.	.20
Sunglasses	3.65

SHOES

Tretorn	25.00
Converse (Size)	19.00
House Shoes	11.00
Beach Combers	2.25
Work Boots	24.00
Giant Shoe Paste	.70
Shoe Paste (Brown)	.50
Shoe Polish	1.35
Laces 27"	.35
Laces 45" (White)	.40
Laces 54" (White)	.40
Insoles	.80

GAMES

Deluxe Chess Set	22.45
Chess Set	6.50
Dominoes	6.25
Deluxe Dominoes	11.75

PRICES SUBJECT TO CHANGE WITHOUT NOTICE ....

Your Unit *May Not Stock ALL Items* Listed....

Remember To Check The Windows and Bulletin Boards at the Commissary for Price Changes and Items out of Stock...

S0870/p2

QUESTURA
DI FORLI'

OGGETTO:Verbale di denuncia di patito furto sporta da:
CATTELAN Maurizio, nato a Padova il 21.9.1960 ivi residente in via U. Foscolo al civico 22/A, domiciliato in Forlì in via Maroncelli al civico nr; 15 tel. 0543/23865.-

L'anno 1991, addì 22 del mese di Marzo alle ore 08.25, negli Uffici della Squadra Mobile della Questura di Forlì.======================
Innanzi a Noi sottoscritti Ufficiali ed Agenti di P.G., appartenent alla suidicata Squadra Mobile, diamo atto che é"presente **CATTELAN M rizio**, in oggetto meglio generalizzato, il quale per ogni effetto d legge denuncia quanto segue:==================================
Ieri sera 21.3.91, parcheggiavo l'auo della mia ragazza **GIAMBI** Patr zia, in questa via P. Maroncelli, alle ore 20.30, la stessa non era chiusa a chiave.L'auto targata FO 453979 e una GOLF WV.===========
========================= All'interno dell'autovettura si trovava u pacep nel cui interno c'era un opera "**INVISIBILE** " la stessa ha un valore affettivo e doveva partecipare ud una mostra a Milano.======
A.D.R.=L'auto, non é assicurata.===================================
A.D.R.=Non ho sospetti su alcuno.==================================

QUESTURA DI FORLI' - SQUADRA MOBILE

A richiesta dell'interessato e per i soli usi consentiti dalla legge si rilascia copia del presente atto.=====================

QUESTURA DI FORLI' - SQUADRA MOBILE

COMUNE DI FORLI'

COMUNE DI FORLI'
...copia, composta di fogli n. 1
...conforme all'originale.
Forlì 02 APR. 1991
IL FUNZIONARIO INCARICATO

On Invisibility in Art
Ralph Rugoff

Despite the immense popularity of mail-order catalogues and phone sex, we still belong to a cultural tradition in which seeing is believing. In the art world, this notion reached an apotheosis of sorts in the early 1960s when Frank Stella formulated his famous credo, 'what you see is what you get', declaring that his paintings comprised nothing besides the paint on the canvas. If Stella's statement seemed to sum up a materialistic strain of artistic activity in the early part of the decade, other artists of the period were not so eager to limit art to what could be perceived visually. In 1968, Barry Le Va, who was then making installations that were plainly visible, declared that the content of his work was, in fact, invisible – its physical elements were merely clues to a meaning which existed elsewhere. Around the same time, a number of conceptual artists began creating intangible projects that eschewed material artefacts. It was an approach summed up in Douglas Huebler's announcement that 'the world is full of objects, more or less interesting. I do not wish to add any more'. It was echoed too in Robert Smithson's belief that 'installations should empty rooms, not fill them', and his suggestion that a museum devoted to different kinds of emptiness could be developed.

previous pages:
pp. 96–97
Billboard poster for Buro Friedrich, Berlin
Liam Gillick
1999

pp. 98–99
Merchandise available on death row in Ellis Unit One, Huntsville, Texas, in 1990

opposite:
Untitled (police report of stolen invisible artwork)
Maurizio Cattelan
1992

The larger background to this flirtation with the imperceptible was the 'bigger is better' aesthetic that characterised so much post-war art: evident in the heroically-sized canvases of Abstract Expressionists, the Pop-giganticism of Rosenquist and Oldenburg, and the monuments of Minimalism and Earth Art. To the aesthetic size-queens associated with these currents, the expansive visibility of an artwork seemingly ensured its public authority and presence. Yet by 1969, invisible art was showing up all over the place. Artist Tom Marioni curated *Invisible Painting and Sculpture* at the Richmond

Art Center in California, for example, which featured a group of artists including Bruce Connor, Michelangelo Pistoletto and Robyn Whitlaw. Robert Barry, who produced works using microwaves, electromagnetic fields, ultrasonic sound and inert gases, summed up a certain strain of interest in the unseen with his 1969 *Telepathic Piece*, which appeared as a bracketed statement in an exhibition catalogue: 'during the exhibition, I will try to communicate telepathically a work of art, the nature of which is a series of thoughts that are not applicable to language or image.'

Telepathic Piece pinpointed a major concern for many artists at the time: an emphasis on thinking and communicative possibilities over art's visible and material qualities. But by invoking a sensibility beyond words, it also underscored an interest in the Sublime – an aesthetic preoccupation which typically gets written out of the Conceptual art story book. For Barry – who once remarked that 'Nothing seems to me the most potent thing in the world' – invisibility was a means of evoking the void and emptiness. Immeasurable and without limit, the realm of the unseen is as Sublime as it gets.

Superficially, the most direct precedent for the invisible art of the 1960s was Yves Klein's romance with the void. Beginning with his 1957 exhibition at Galerie Colette Allendy, which included an empty white room saturated with what the artist called 'invisible pictorial sensibility', Klein embarked on a utopian programme of producing immaterial art, establishing zones of immateriality (and selling them), presenting 'invisible paintings' at group exhibitions and drawing up plans for an 'architecture of the air' – including an 'air roof', designed to serve as a transparent shield over habitats and large tracts of land. For Klein, the great benefit of invisible architecture was that it would enable people to maintain constant visual contact with the sky, and so to retain a connection to its sublime expanses. A desire to instil a similar sensation of unboundedness also informed exhibitions such as *Le Vide* of 1958, for which he removed all objects from Iris Clert's Parisian gallery except for an empty vitrine. Although the space appeared unoccupied and devoid of content, Klein insisted that it was filled with the medium of human consciousness: a force so tangible that, according to the artist, some people were unable to enter the exhibition as if an invisible wall prevented them.

Klein predicated such works on his belief that our perception of art does not depend on vision or any other physical sense, but on what he called 'sensibility' or 'affectivity', terms which vaguely conjure up realms of unfettered imagination and emotion. But in the 1960s, these shop-worn trademarks of the Sublime were given short shrift by a new generation of invisible works. Art & Language, for example, designated the volume of air in an empty air-conditioned gallery as an artwork, not in order to provoke an experience of unbounded awareness but to argue (as Duchamp had with found objects) that art, rather than being an identifiable through specific visual characteristics, is defined by its cultural and conceptual context. As they declared in a 1968 essay: 'things are noticed and attended to not in virtue of some "naturally" obvious assertiveness but in respect of culturally, instrumentally, and materially conditioned discursive activity.'

In the sphere of public art, disillusionment with traditional political monuments gave birth to what art historian Sergiusz Michalski has called 'a new art form: monuments which tried to attain invisibility as a way of engendering reflection on the limitations of monumental imagery'. Curiously, Claes Oldenburg, better known for the wry giganticism of his homages to everyday objects, played a leading role in developing this low-profile territory. His *Proposed Underground Memorial and Tomb for President John F Kennedy* (1965) called for a huge statue of the assassinated President to be buried head-first in the ground. The statue's size would be identical to that of the Statue of Liberty, suggesting that Kennedy's murder had turned the American Dream on its head. In 1967, Oldenburg actually carried out a proposal for a very different kind of invisible monument – one intended to protest not only against the Vietnam War but also the celebratory heroic memorials that the artist imagined (wrongly as it turned out) would eventually be erected to honour its veterans. For *Placid Civil Monument* (1967), Oldenburg hired a crew of municipal grave-diggers to excavate a hole in the lawn behind New York's Metropolitan Museum of Art. Besides suggesting a grave, the hole evoked an inverted plinth, cancelling out in advance the visibility of future monuments to the war. But *Placid Civil Monument* ultimately went beyond the negative iconography of the Kennedy memorial, as the artist, after documenting the grave-diggers' work, had the hole filled in, leaving no trace of its brief existence.

The same year, Maria Nordman began creating works in specific urban settings, usually in and around Los Angeles, that employed ambient sounds, shifting sunlight and shadow, and the chance presence of local pedestrians. Geared towards accidental encounters and blending with their surrounding environments, Nordman's works ideally attained a kind of invisible participation in the flow of urban life: an aesthetic which seemingly matched her desire to create a democratic art that would be accessible to viewers from all backgrounds. The idealistic undertones of Nordman's approach resonate in much other invisible art from this period, as if practitioners believed their work could achieve a state of social and political grace simply by dispensing with a perceptible presence. From another perspective, however, projects like Nordman's represent the culmination of a century-long concern with dissolving the boundaries between the work of art and its larger environment – a vein of interest that essentially reverses the strategy of collage: rather than incorporating wordly fragments, the artwork is incorporated into its surrounding milieu, embracing a dissolution of identity that, once again, recalls the mechanisms of the Sublime.

For later artists, idealism took a back seat and invisibility became a strategy for provoking and frustrating audiences, and playing against their expectations, by withholding the anticipated object of desire. For *Oh Dracula*, a 1974 performance at the Utah Museum of Art in Salt Lake City, Chris Burden replaced a painting on the wall with a large cloth chrysalis which he then climbed inside. Burden hung on the wall for one day during museum hours, cloistered in darkness like a light-sensitive vampire. In *White Light/White Heat* (1975), the artist spent three weeks concealing himself from viewers in a New York gallery, lying on a wide shelf-like platform which he had built high enough so that he was hidden from view. Burden commented at the time that he was curious to find out whether people would be able to sense his unseen presence, and, no doubt, whether they would really believe he was there if they couldn't actually see him.

Playing on the spectator's good faith, these invisible performances wryly replaced the avant-garde's traditional hostility towards its audience with a passive/aggressive withholding. In the early 1960s, Duchamp had proclaimed his disgust at the commercialisation of the art world, declaring that 'the only solution for the great artist of tomorrow is to go underground' – to become invisible. Works such as Burden's, which were less about invisibility *per se* than about something being hidden from view, inevitably raised questions about the place of art – and the artist – in a commodity-driven culture of over exposure, even as they seemed to throw back into the public's face accusations that contemporary art was merely a case of the Emperor's New Clothes.

Hiding oneself or one's art can also be an exercise in humility, an ego-stripping practice designed to force artist and audience alike to rethink the desire to exhibit, and to question the narcissistic value we place on public approbation in general. The performance artist Tehching Hsieh, probably best known for the year-long performances he began in the 1970s (such as living outdoors in New York City for a twelve-month period) has recently completed such a project but, by its nature, it would be surprising if many people were aware that he had even embarked upon it. For a thirteen-year performance which stretched from 31 December 1986 until 31 December 1999, Hsieh continued to make art, but did not show it to anyone in any way, shape or form. The lesson in invisibility he offers is simple yet powerful: rather than take the measure of himself from the external world, he makes do with his own internal value system – a system which remains unseen but must be deeply felt in order to carry out such a project.

Invisible art continued to reappear at odd intervals during the 1980s and 1990s, typically in a more ironic mode. Andy Warhol, Mr Visibility himself, produced and installed his 1985 *Invisible Sculpture* at New York's Area nightclub – a place where people went to be seen – by stepping on a plinth and stepping off it, presumably leaving traces of his resonant celebrity aura orbiting in its airspace. Almost a decade later, Tom Friedman made what could be seen – if only you could see it – as a distinctly non-utopian return to Klein's practice of 'sensibilising' space. Hiring a professional witch, Friedman instructed her to cast a curse on a spherical space floating 27cm above the top of a pedestal, which the artist subsequently exhibited as *Untitled (Cursed Space)*, a droll inversion of the quasi-theological aura created by museum and gallery display rhetoric.

A number of other artists in the 1990s have explored a slacker-style, degree-zero dissolution that often flirts with notions of invisibility. For her 1996 performance *Invisible Crowds*, Hayley Newman dispersed her audience of fifty by bus to unannounced locations across Vancouver and left them to find their own way home. In 1990, Peter Santino began a ten-year project entitled *Failure* (in the astronomical sense of the word, which refers to gravitational collapse) for which he produced series of tiny lead balls that grew ever smaller over the course of the decade, culminating in a group of invisible works planned for 2000.

When architectural showpieces such as the Guggenheim Bilbao or the new Tate Modern attract more attention than the artworks they house, and when curators are spurred to create ever more spectacular exhibitions to compete with such spaces, the idea of invisible art can serve as a much-needed tonic, prompting us to see through the art world's grandiose distractions, and so, perhaps, to think a little more clearly. They also remind us that, in the larger scheme of things, art occupies a fairly immaterial position, and whether visible or not, works of art ultimately come to life only in our imaginations, in the unseen museums we carry within us.

But perhaps the most salutary effect of invisible art lies in the chameleon-like array of meanings which have cloaked it over the past half century. Rather than simply serving as a static limit defining the no-go zone of artistic practice, it has alternately appeared under the guise of the Sublime, of social idealism, avant-garde aggression, personal humility and ironic commentary. No single artist has been able to possess invisibility as a signature medium, and its wayward history gently yet pointedly mocks our waning belief in the cult of originality. It suggests instead that art doesn't begin and end in a physical frame or a singular context, but lives on in the potentially endless process by which we make use of it.

opposite:
Understudy A
Gaia Alessi
1999

overleaf:
Untitled
Robert Barry
1971

Robert Barry

it can be presented,
experienced,
defined,
placed,
first,
last,
changed,
described,
interpreted,
integrated,
sustained,
clarified,
confined,
attached,
attacked,
defended,
conditioned,
delineated,
replaced,
questioned,
explained,
limited,
established,
unified,
separated,
present,
absent,
unknown,
effected,
effectual,
announced,
recognised,
concealed,
believed,
avoided,
rejected,
contradicted,
affirmed,
remembered,
forgotten,
interesting,
specific,
anywhere,
missing,
featured,

influential,
accessible,
assimilated,
independent,
noticed,
ignored,
mundane,
lost,
found,
discussed,
disbursed,
destroyed,
improved,
removed,
continued,
alone,
near,
remote,
denied,
neglected,
discovered,
purposeful,
directed,
free,
predicted,
public,
private,
allowed,
repeated,
anticipated,
accepted,
familiar,
strange,
prevented,
doubted,
followed,
and completed.

1971

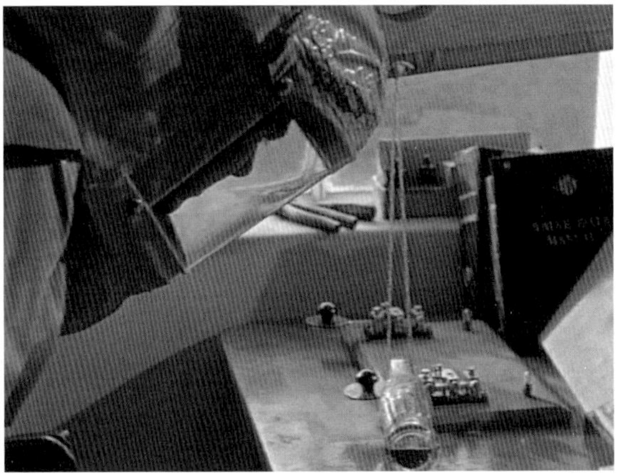

In the aftermath of a global nuclear conflict (which will eventually destroy the human race), a US Navy officer searches for survivors, and then discovers a cruel turn of fate. What his party had thought was some kind of distress signal turns out to be the work of the wind, a Coke bottle and a stray piece of cord from a window blind...

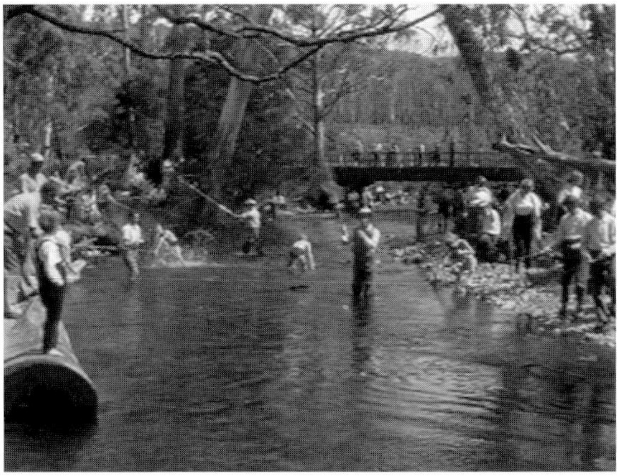

Later in the film, as a lethal radiation cloud approaches and survivors of the first onslaught are faced with counting down the last days and hours of their lives, the inhabitants of a small town in Australia gather together by a river.
On The Beach director Stanley Kramer (1959)

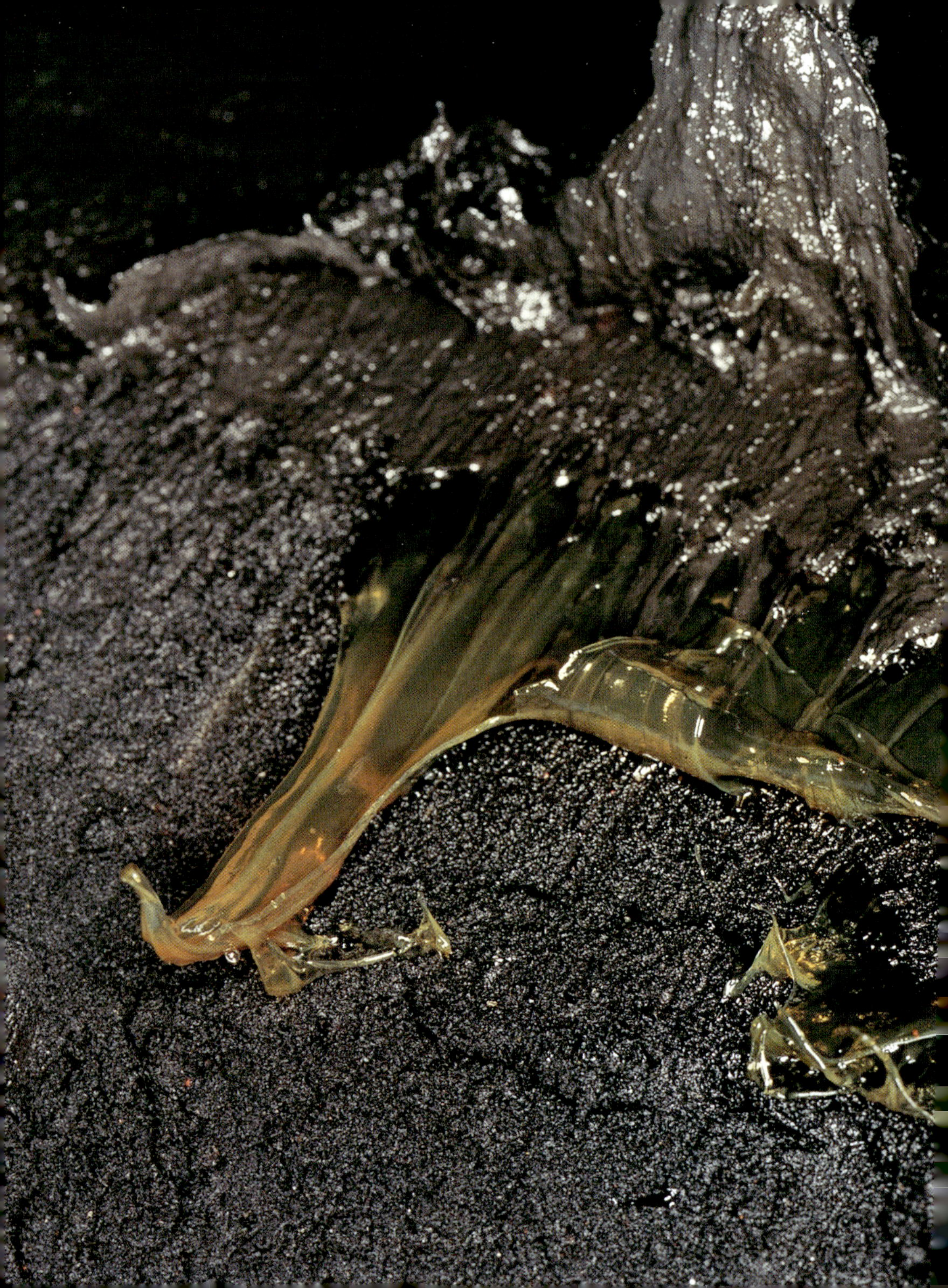

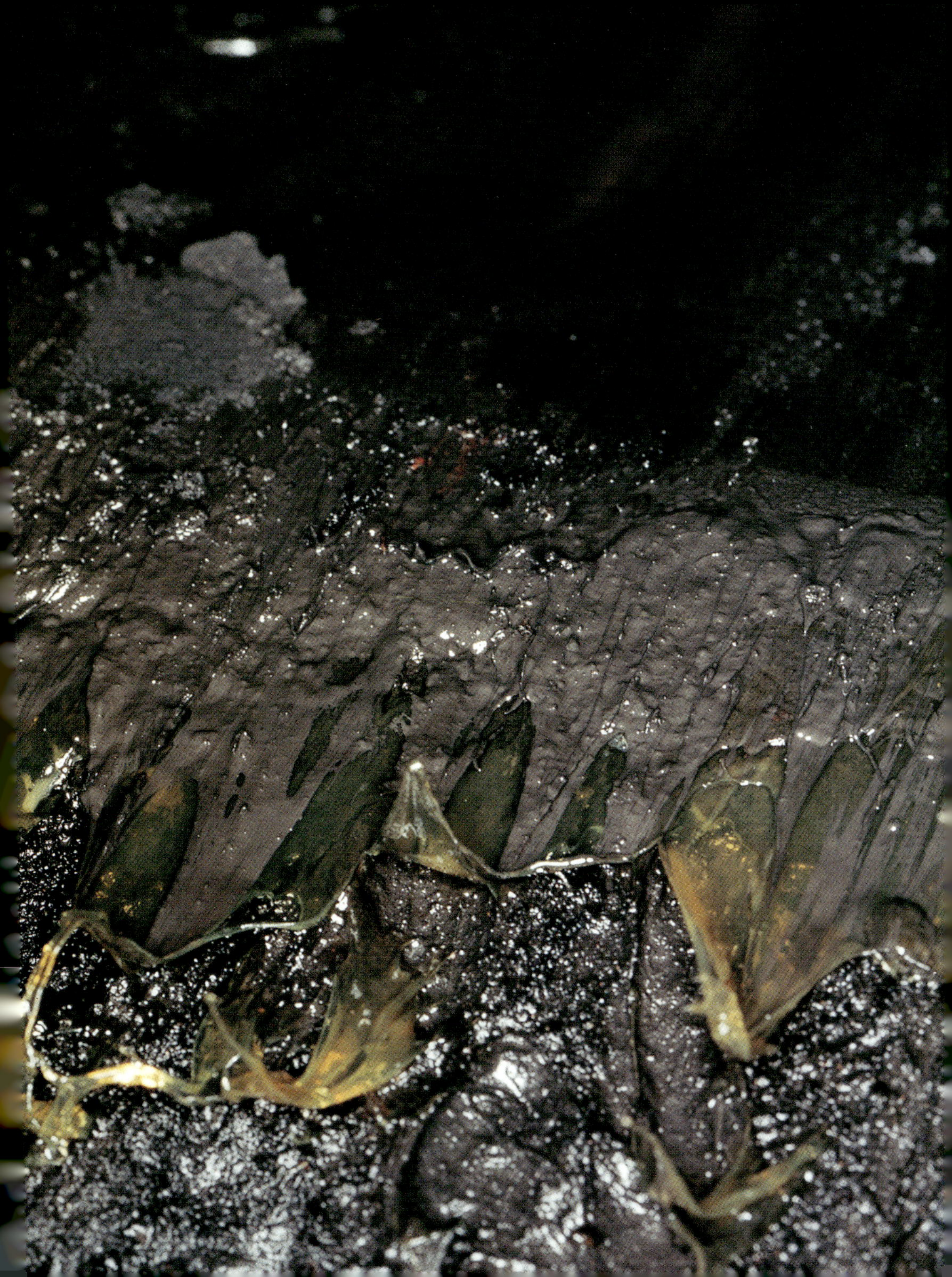

previous spread:
Untitled
(from the series 'Material')
Peter Fraser
2000

below:
Untitled
(from the series 'Material')
Peter Fraser
2000

opposite:
Solaris
(cover of 1973 edition)

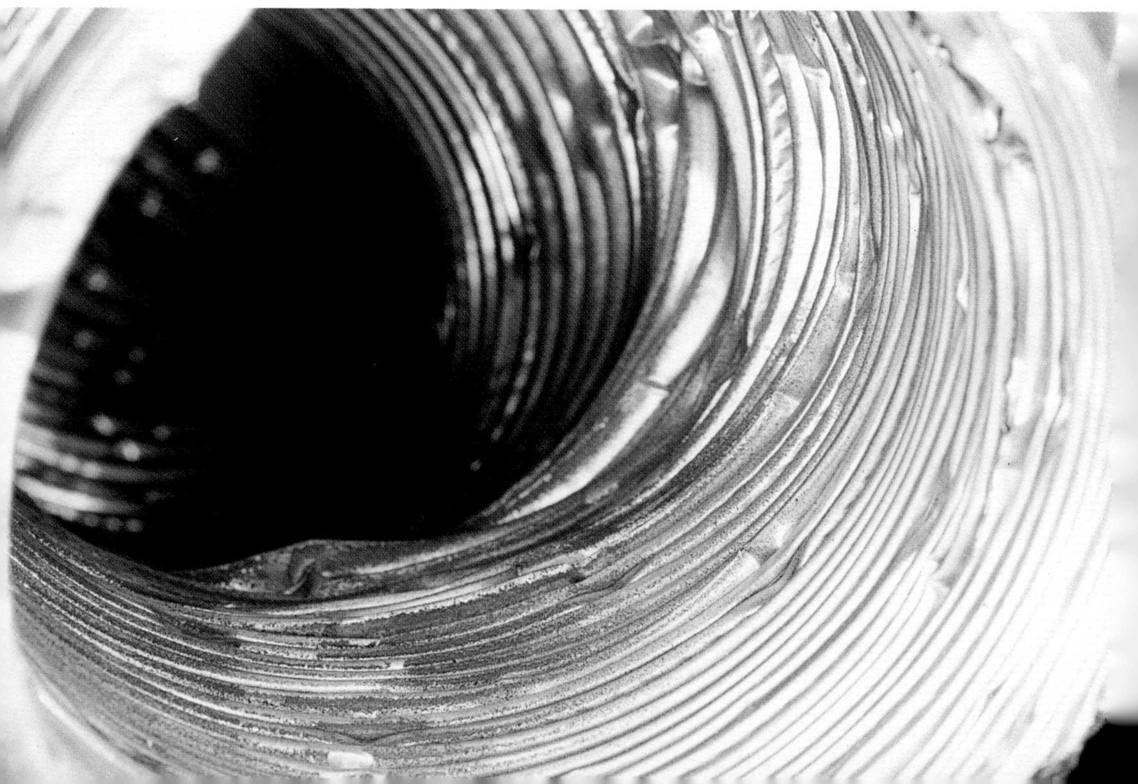

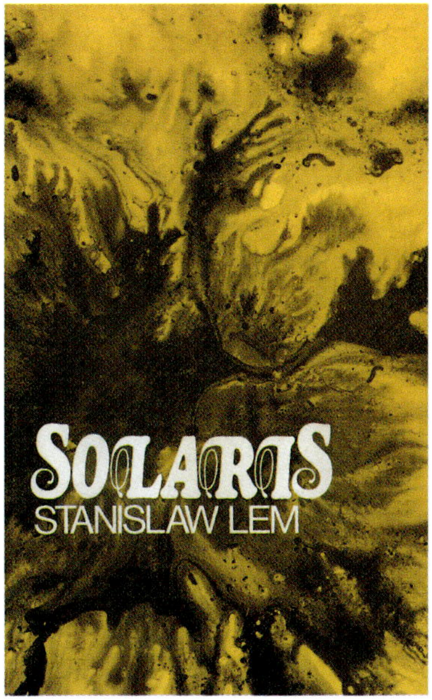

Written by Stanislaw Lem in 1961, *Solaris* depicts a planet entirely covered by a vast, liquid expanse, a 'plasmic ocean' which seems to possess intelligence.

In the book, it is described as a 'sort of gigantic entity, a fluid cell, unique and monstrous, surrounding the globe with a colloidal envelope'. Constantly shifting and creating fantastic edifices which congeal, then break up and become fluid again, the ocean is characterised as a huge formless mass. This formlessness becomes terrifying to the scientists who study it. Attempting to understand the ocean's qualities and its activity, they are driven half mad with incomprehension – unable to decide whether the 'monstrous' nothingness with which they are confronted is a sentient being or material that has no meaning.

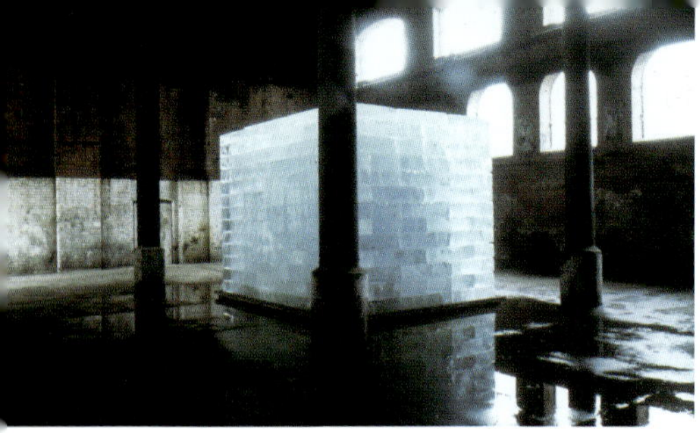
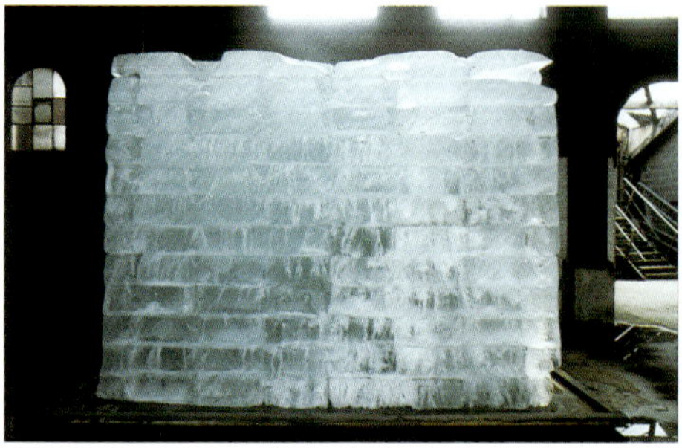
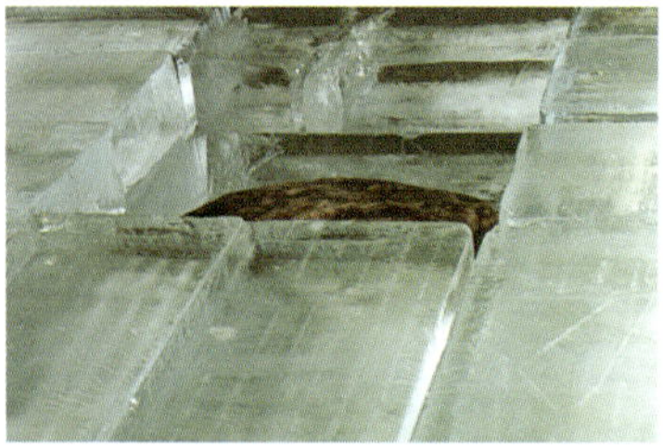
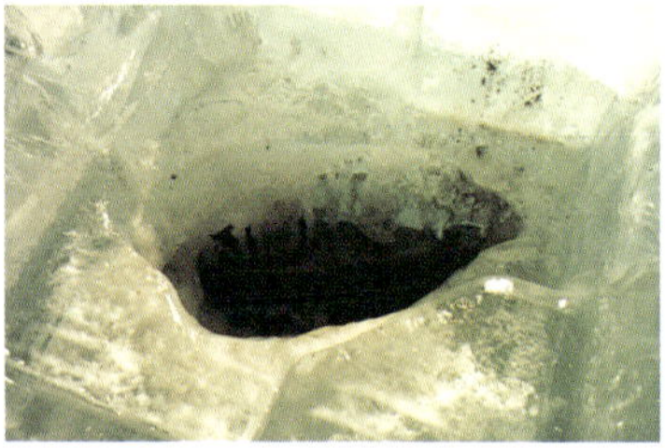
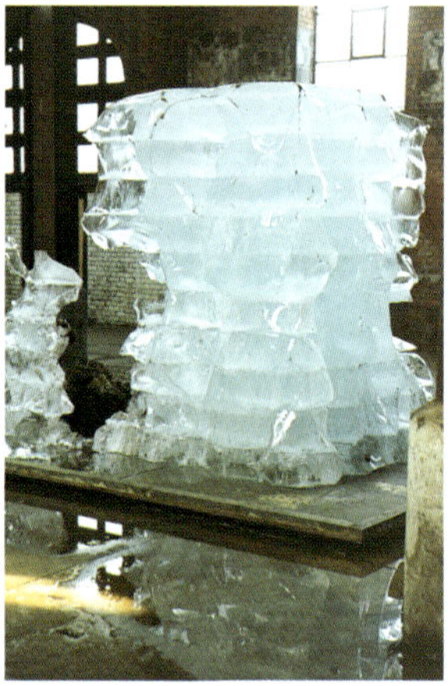
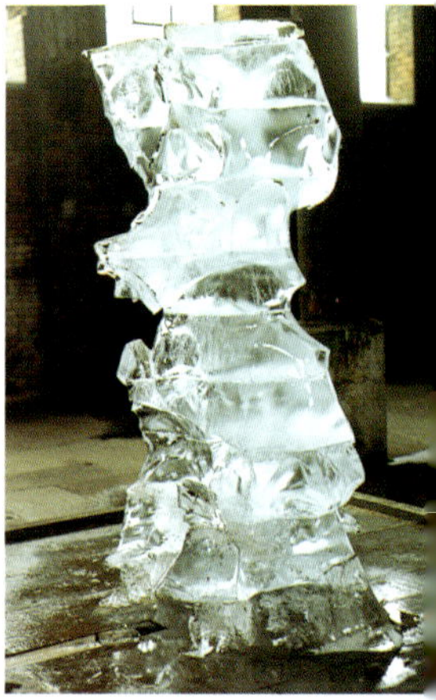
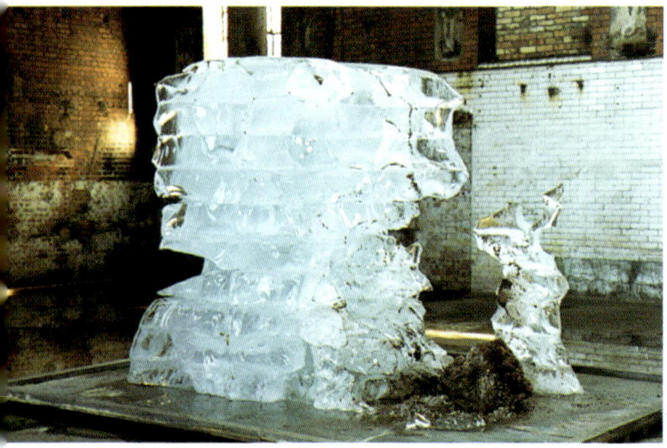
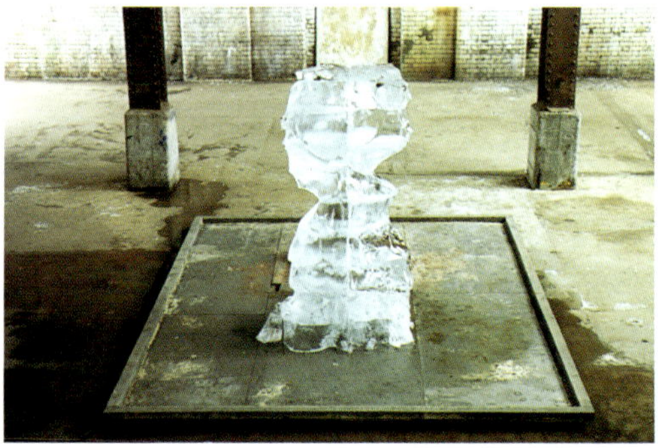
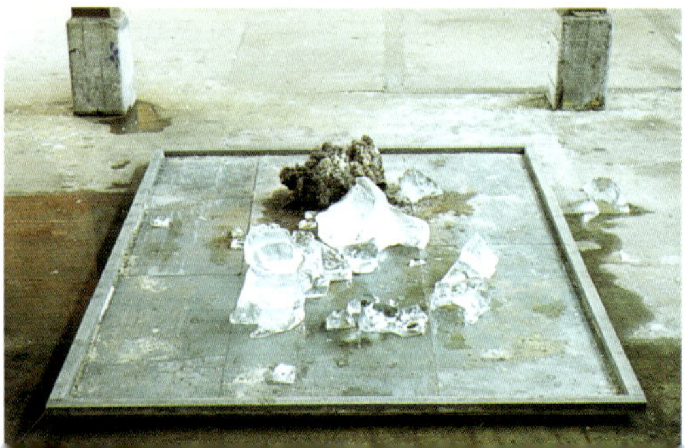
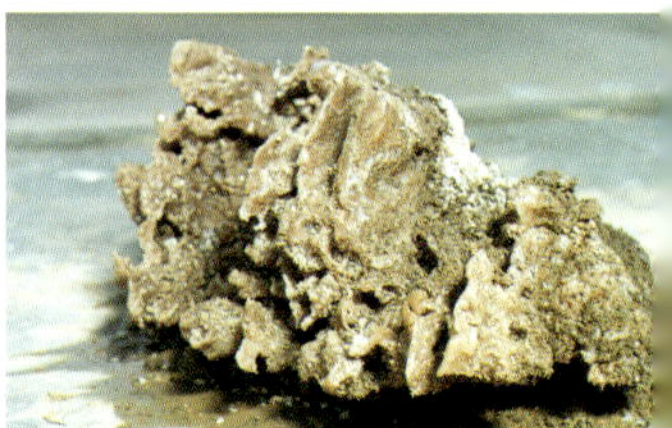

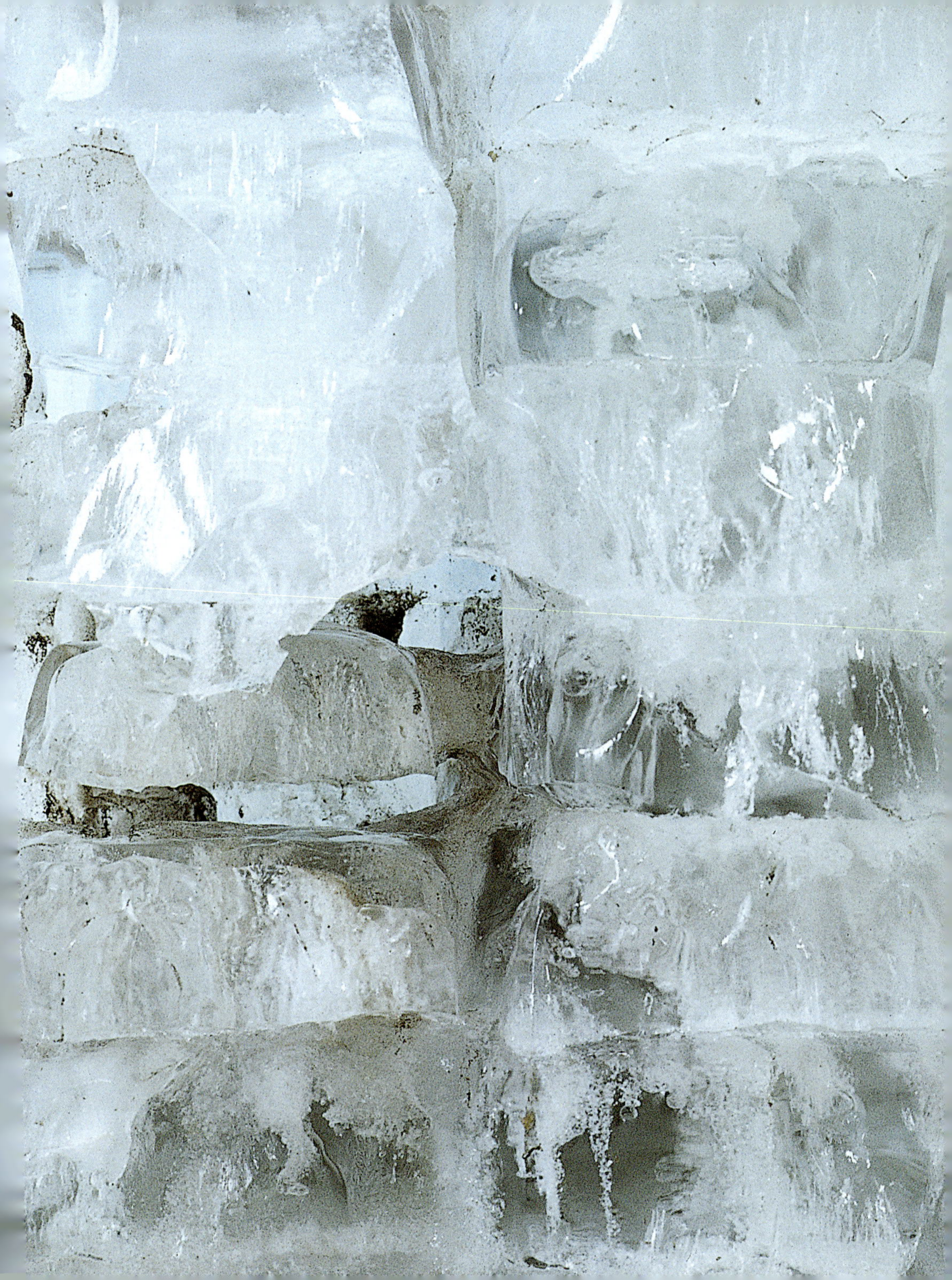

previous spread:
Intensities and Surfaces
Anya Gallaccio
1996

below:
Conical Intersect
(still)
Gordon Matta-Clark
1975

opposite:
Nothing 1
Angela de la Cruz
1998

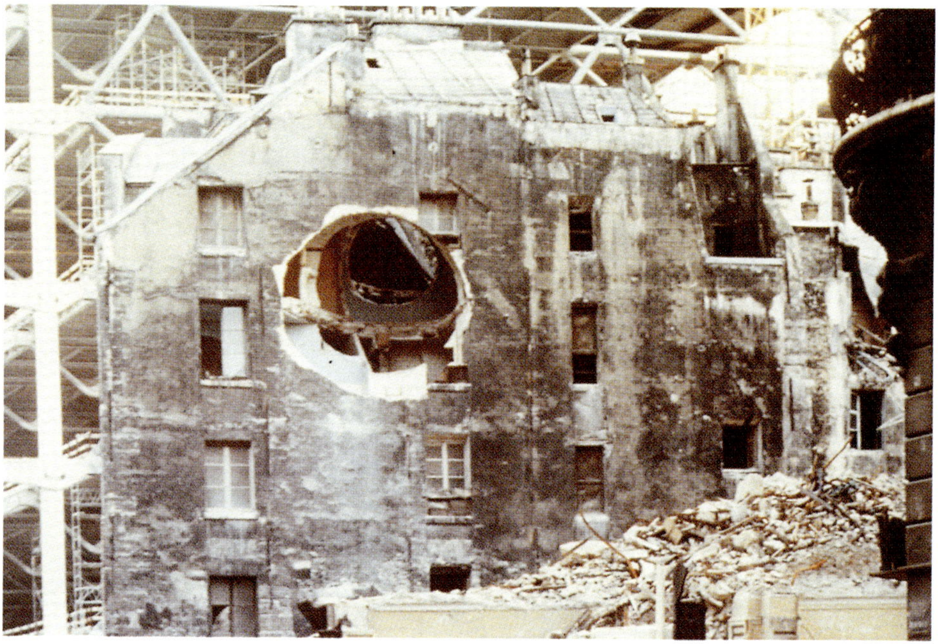

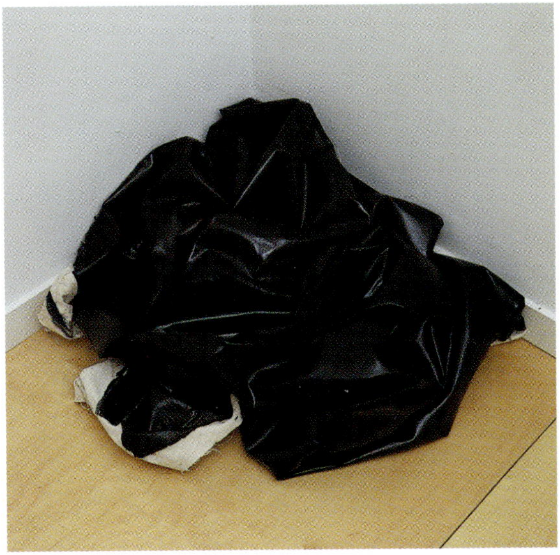

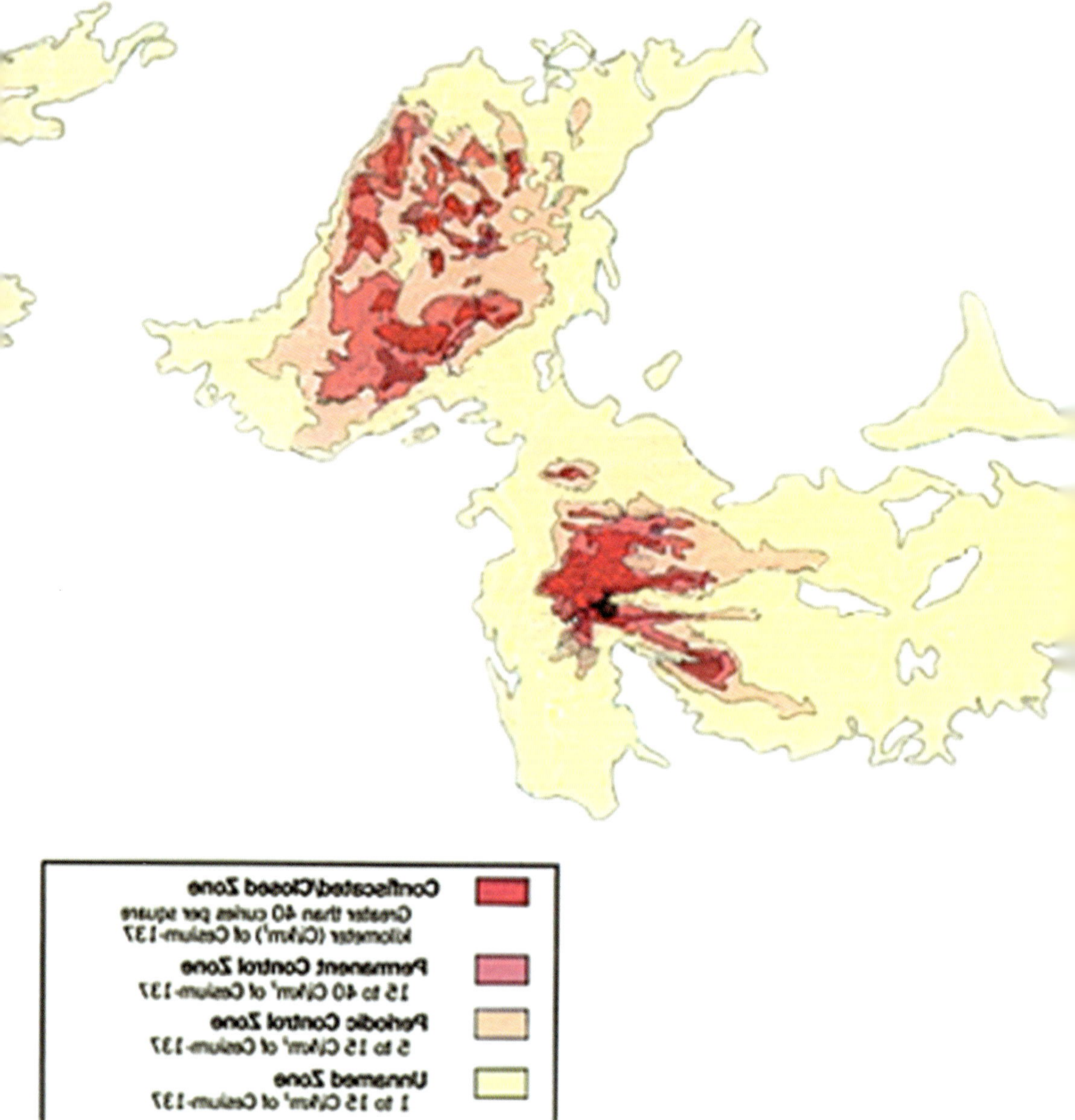
Confiscated/Closed Zone
Greater than 40 curies per square kilometer (Ci/km²) of Cesium-137
Permanent Control Zone
15 to 40 Ci/km² of Cesium-137
Periodic Control Zone
5 to 15 Ci/km² of Cesium-137
Unnamed Zone
1 to 15 Ci/km² of Cesium-137

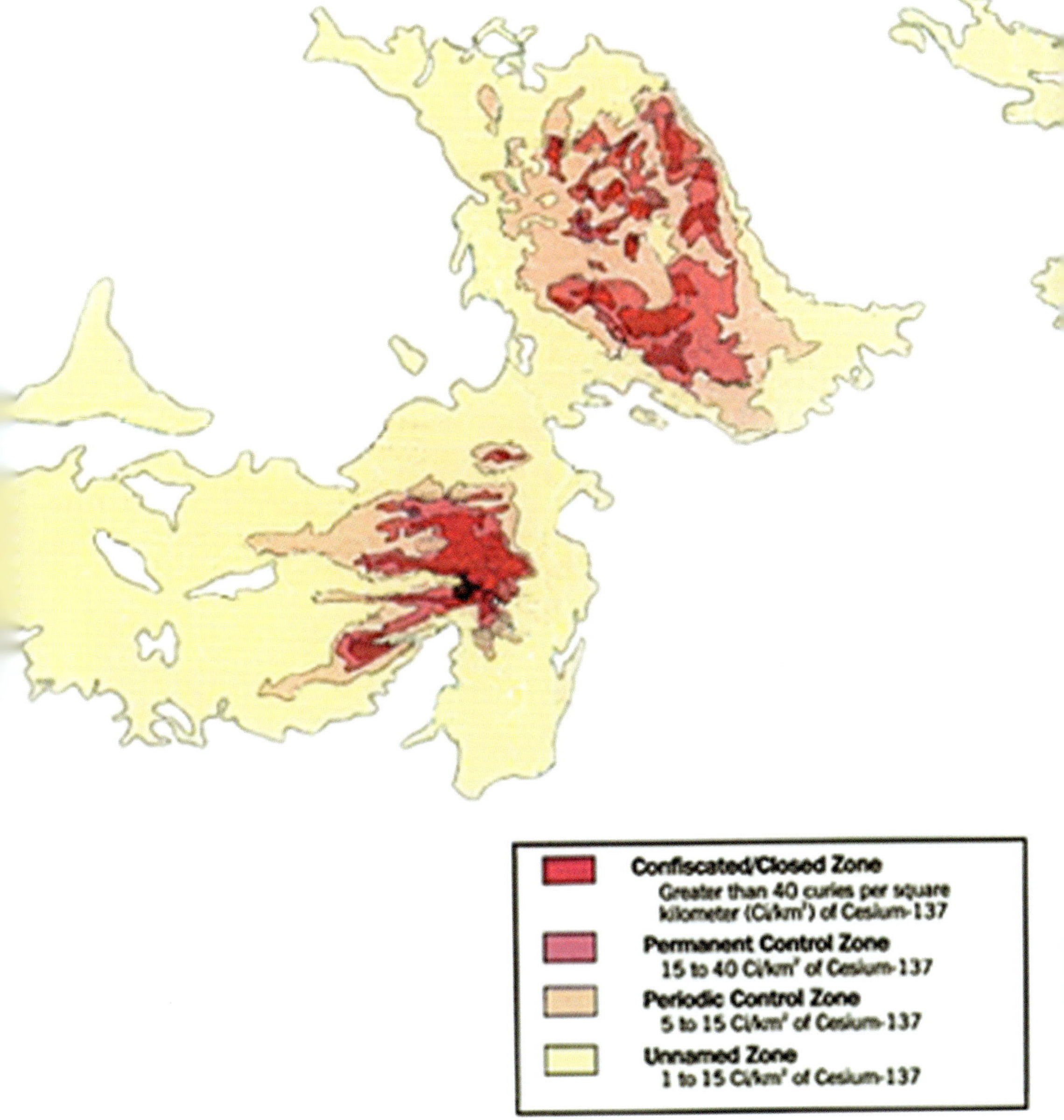
Confiscated/Closed Zone
Greater than 40 curies per square kilometer (Ci/km²) of Cesium-137
Permanent Control Zone
15 to 40 Ci/km² of Cesium-137
Periodic Control Zone
5 to 15 Ci/km² of Cesium-137
Unnamed Zone
1 to 15 Ci/km² of Cesium-137

previous spread:
That Feeling You Get
Richard Bradbury
2000

below:
Garbage Bag
Ceal Floyer
1996

opposite:
LAP Project
AL: Charlotte Cullinan + Jeanine Richards
1998

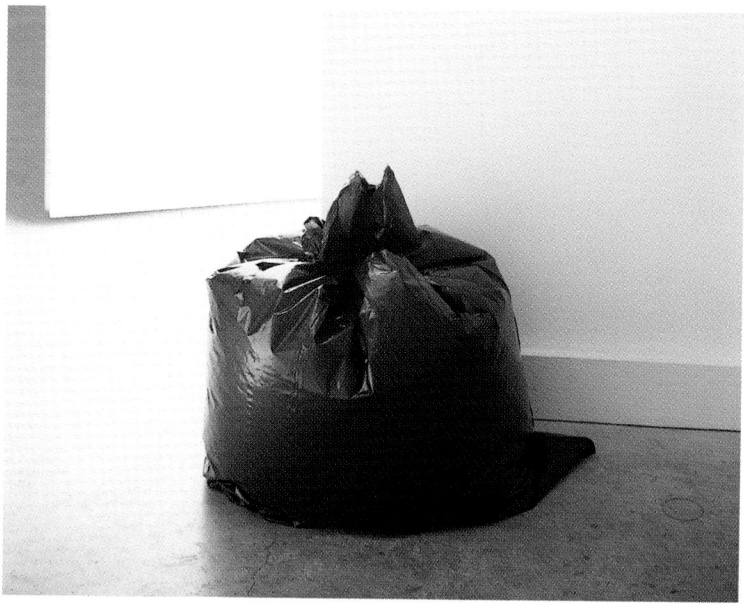

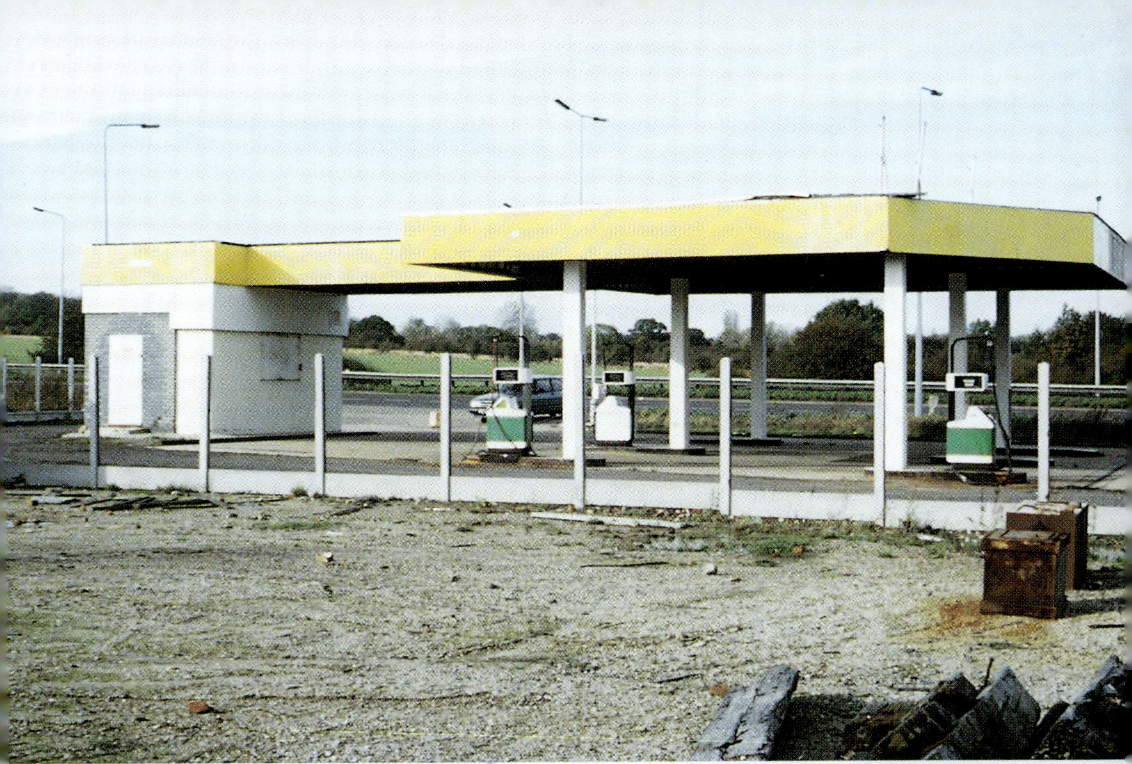
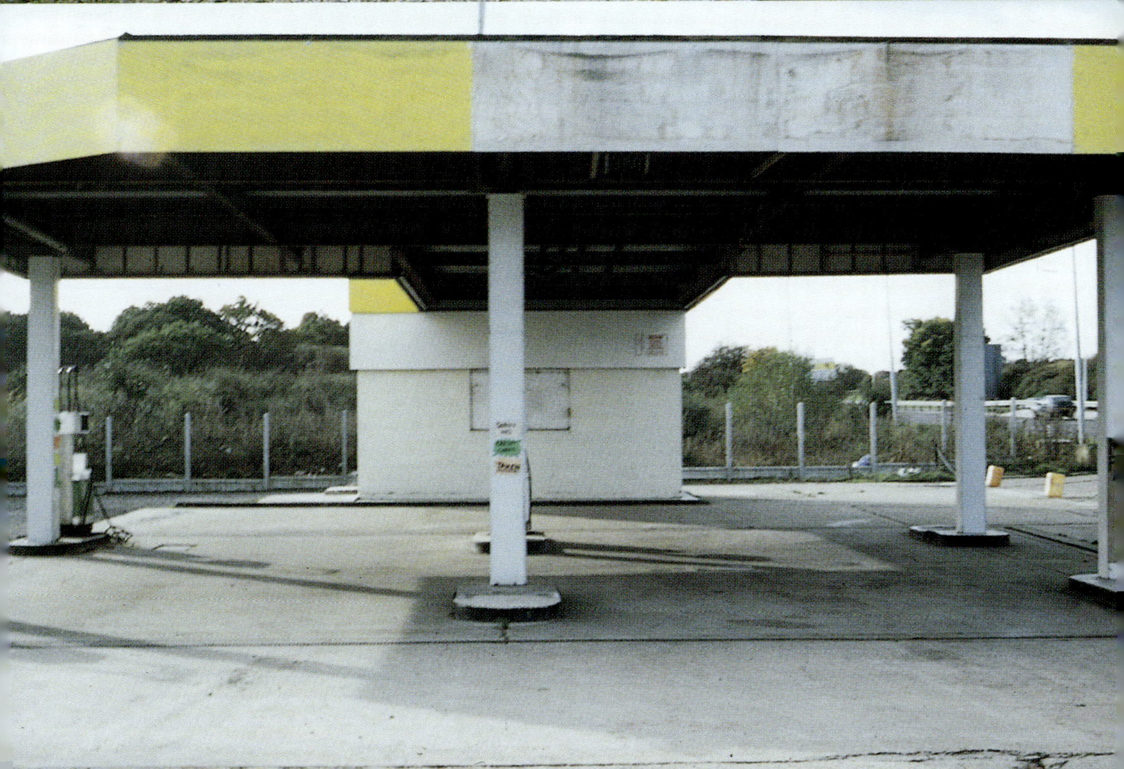

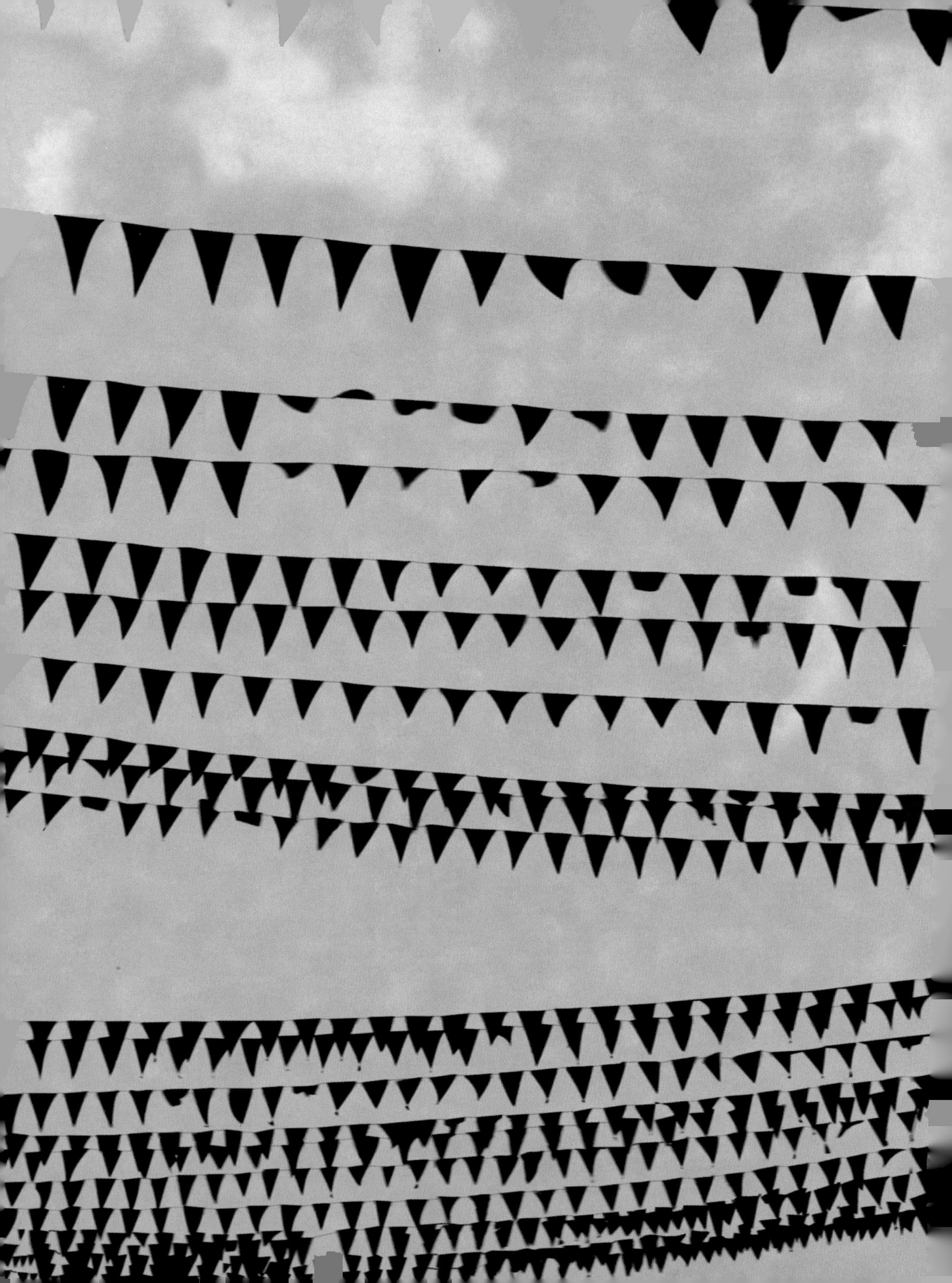

opposite:
Black Bunting
Fiona Banner
2001

below:
Closed
Jonathan Monk
1996

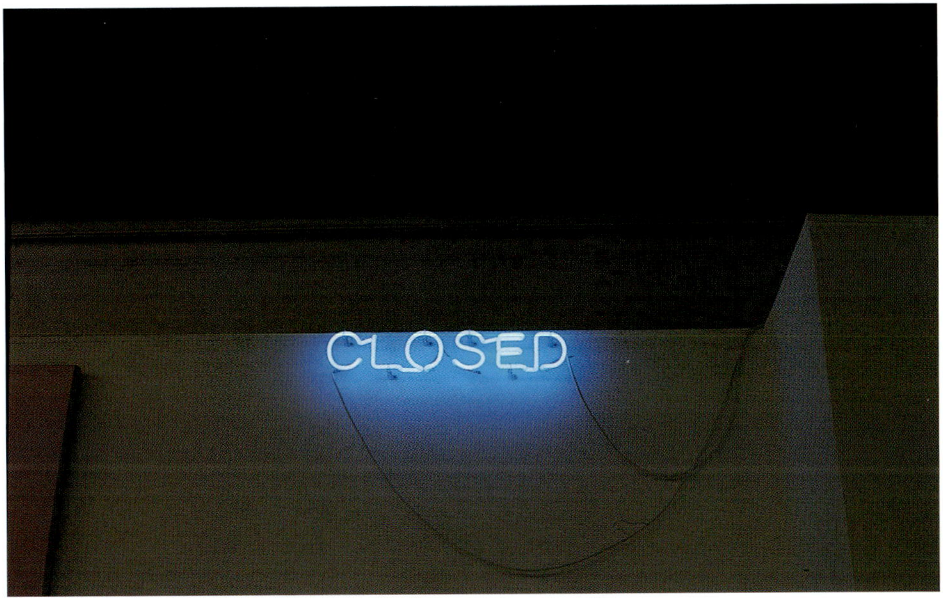

Puddle is an ordinary urban puddle, made by lifting and re-laying an area of paving so that should it rain, a puddle will form. Its exact whereabouts are not disclosed. At the end of the period of exhibition, *Puddle* is removed by restoring the original lie of the slabs.

Keith Wilson, 1999

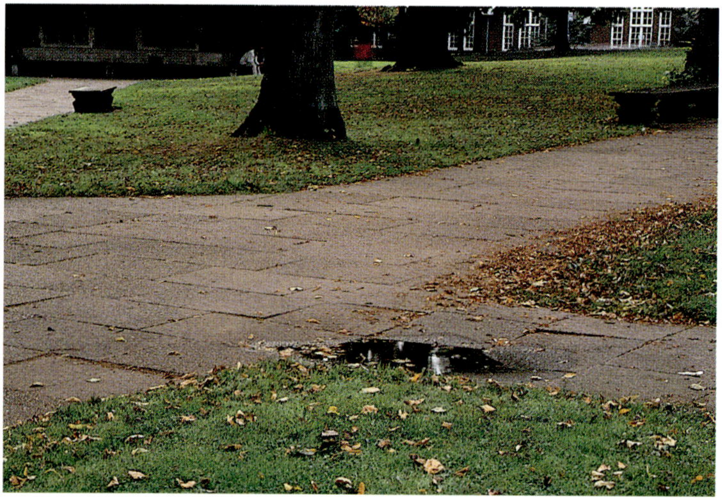

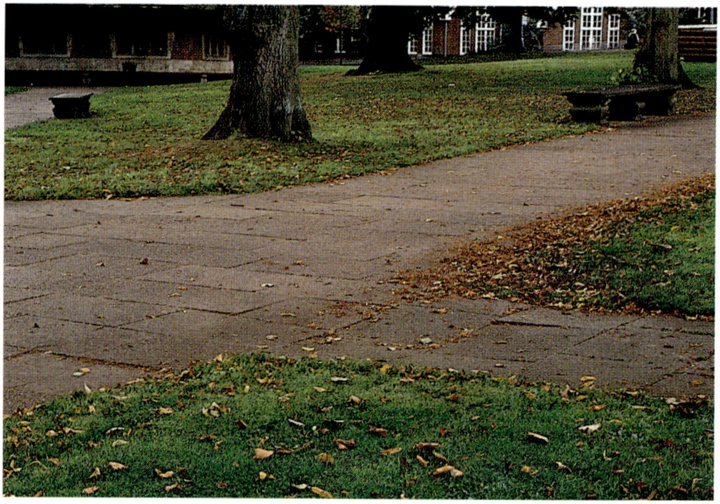

below:
Time Landscape
(documentary photo)
Alan Sonfist
(ongoing) New York

overleaf:
Drain
Robert Gober
1989

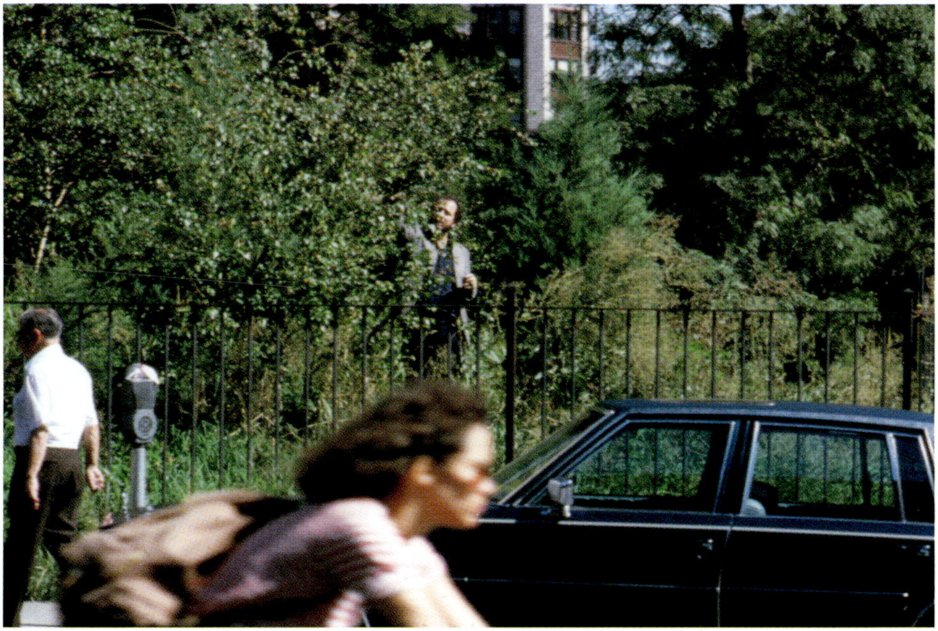

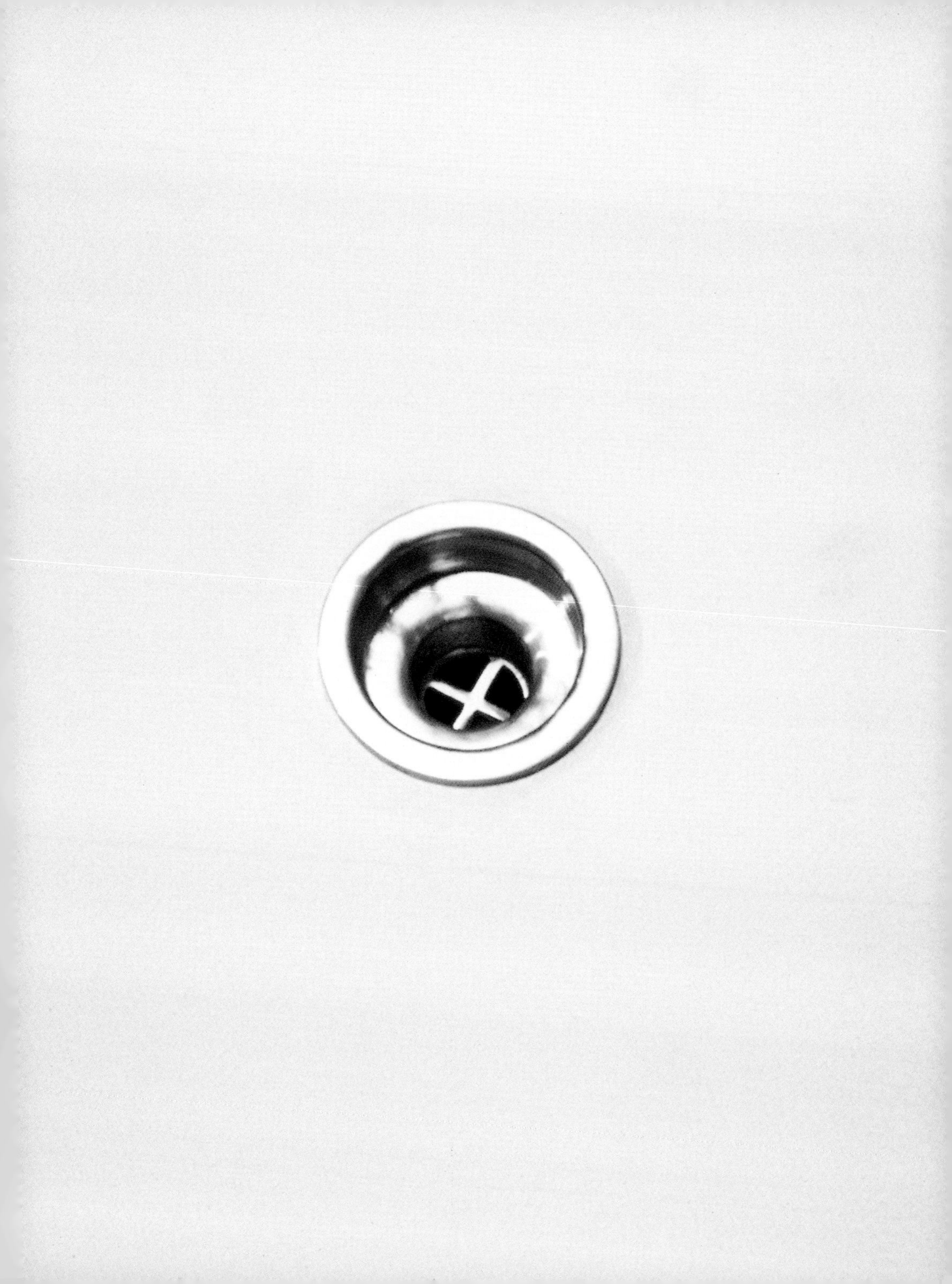

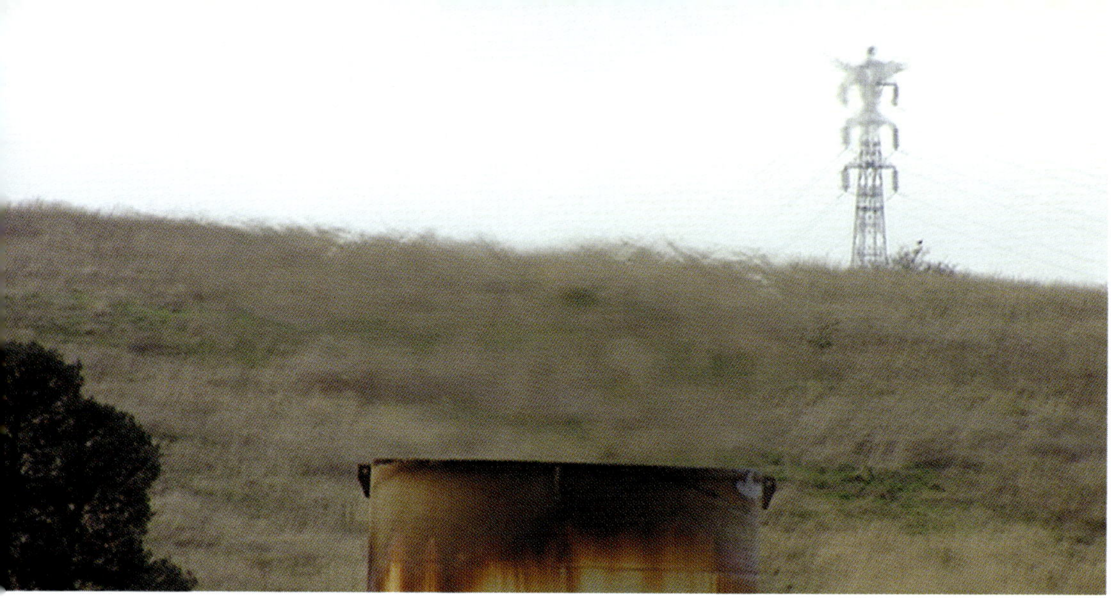

above:
The Dilapidated Dwelling (still)
Patrick Keiller
for Channel 4
2000

opposite:
Film of me hiding in the bushes (still)
Matthew Crawley
1996

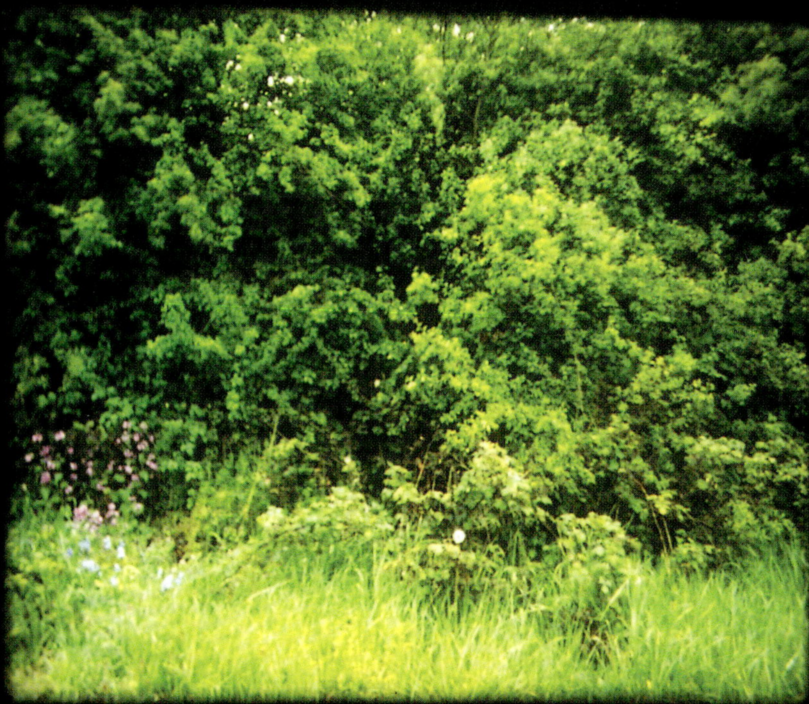

below:
220V, 2.2kW
(production shot)
Andrew Weir
2000

opposite:
Strollology,
Cloud Walk 7,
6 January 1998
Gerhard Lang

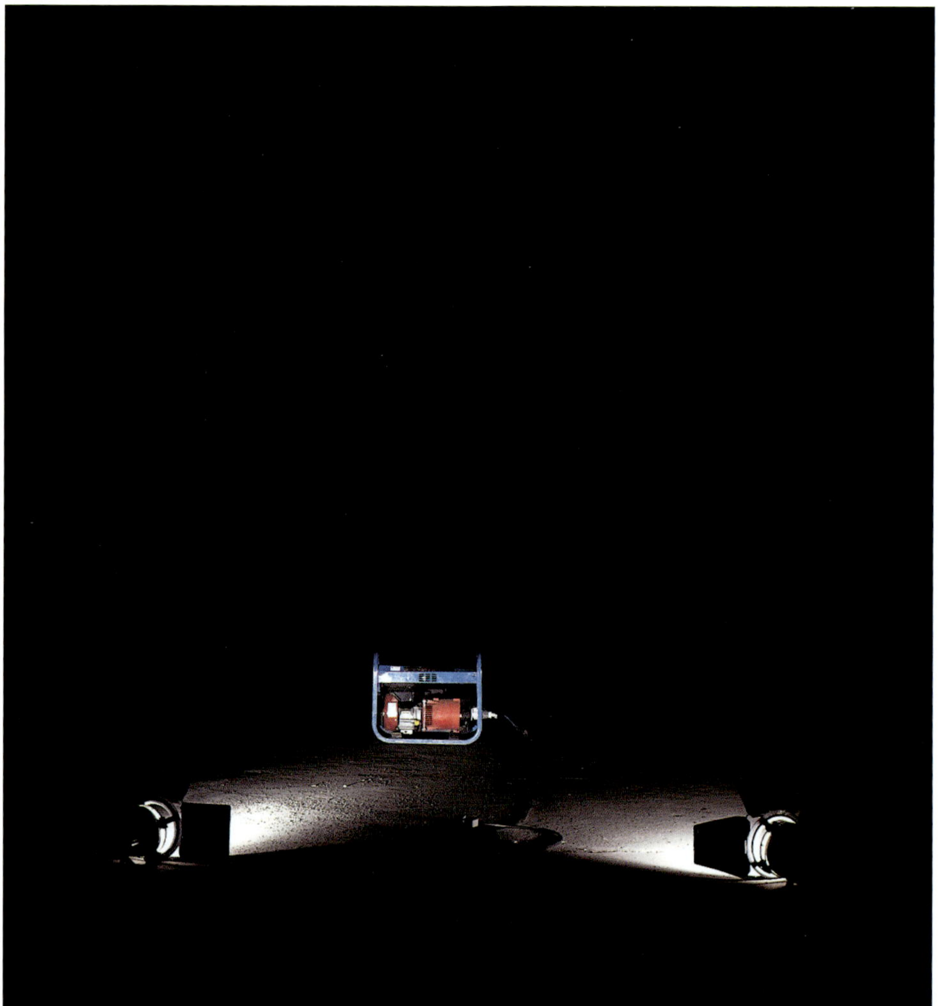

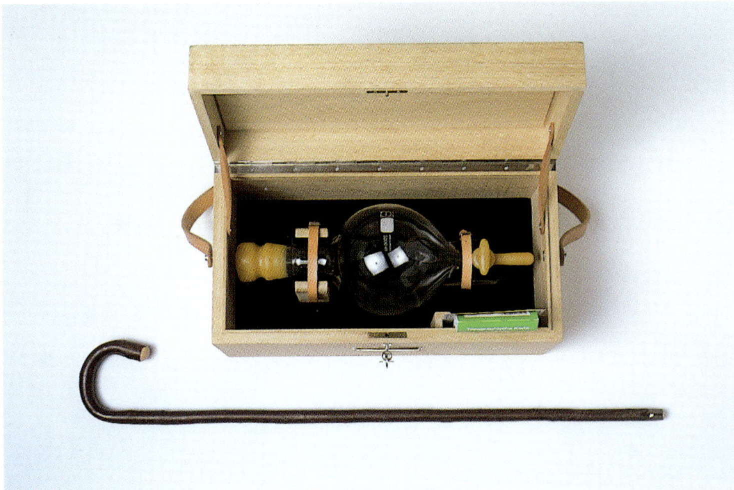

Sometimes Making Nothing Leads to Something
Mexico, DF 2000
Francis Alÿs

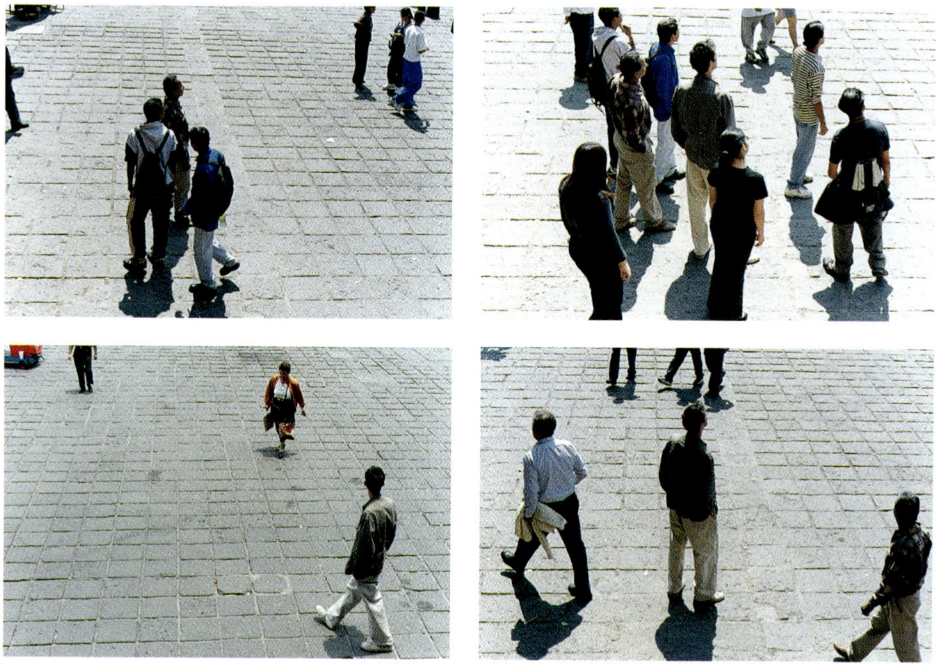

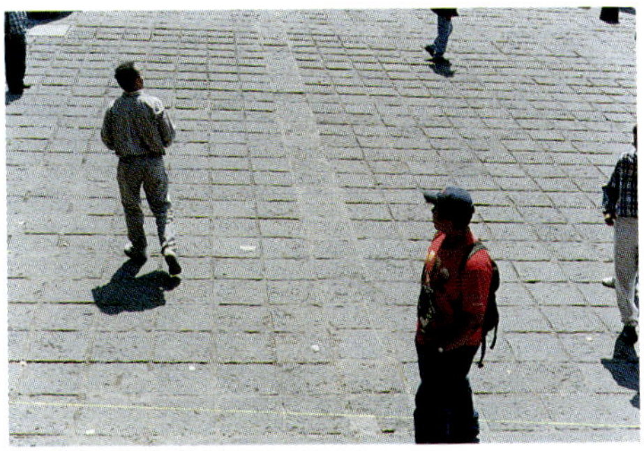

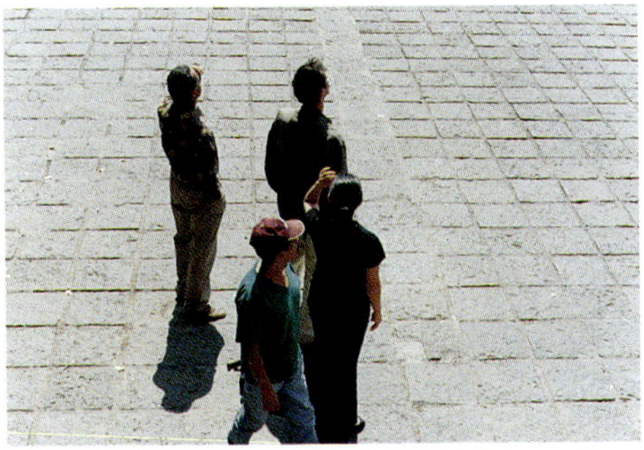

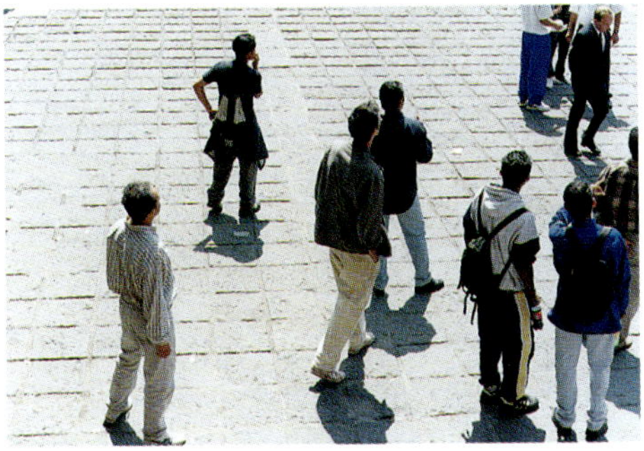

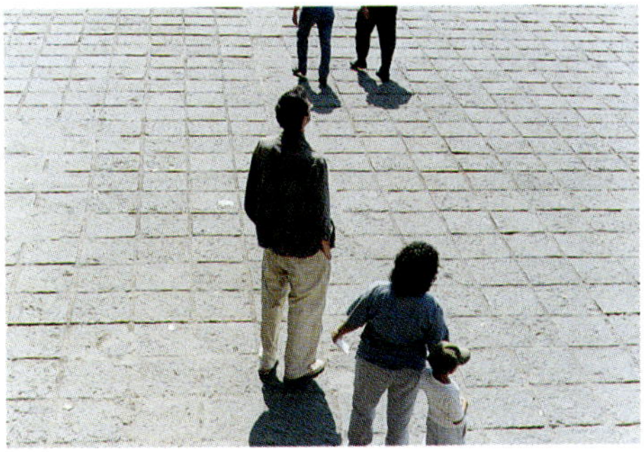

Sometimes Making Something Leads to Nothing
Mexico, DF 1997
Francis Alÿs

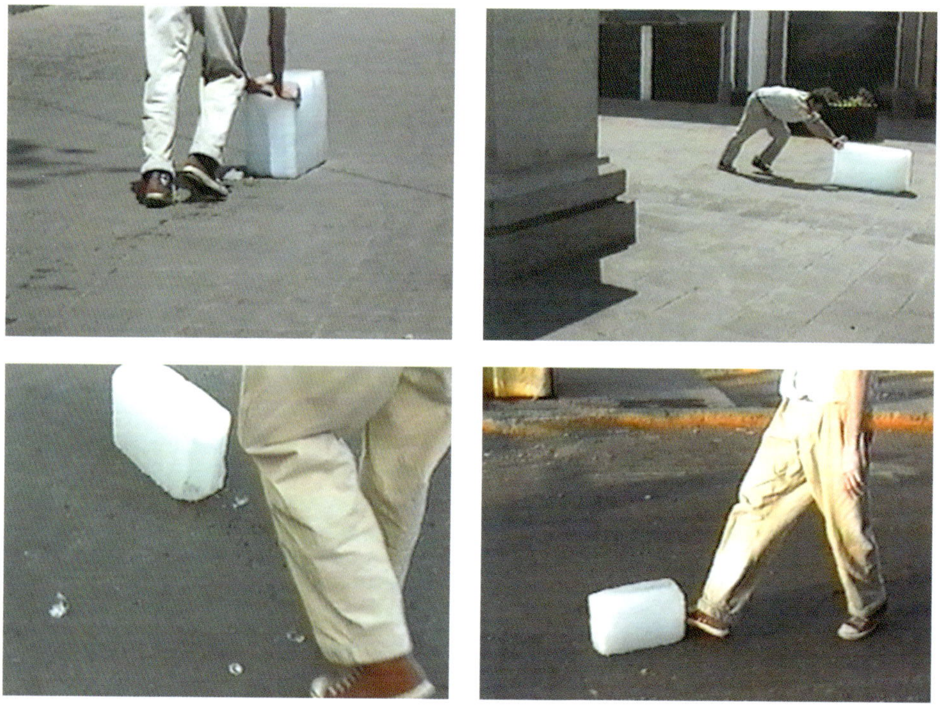

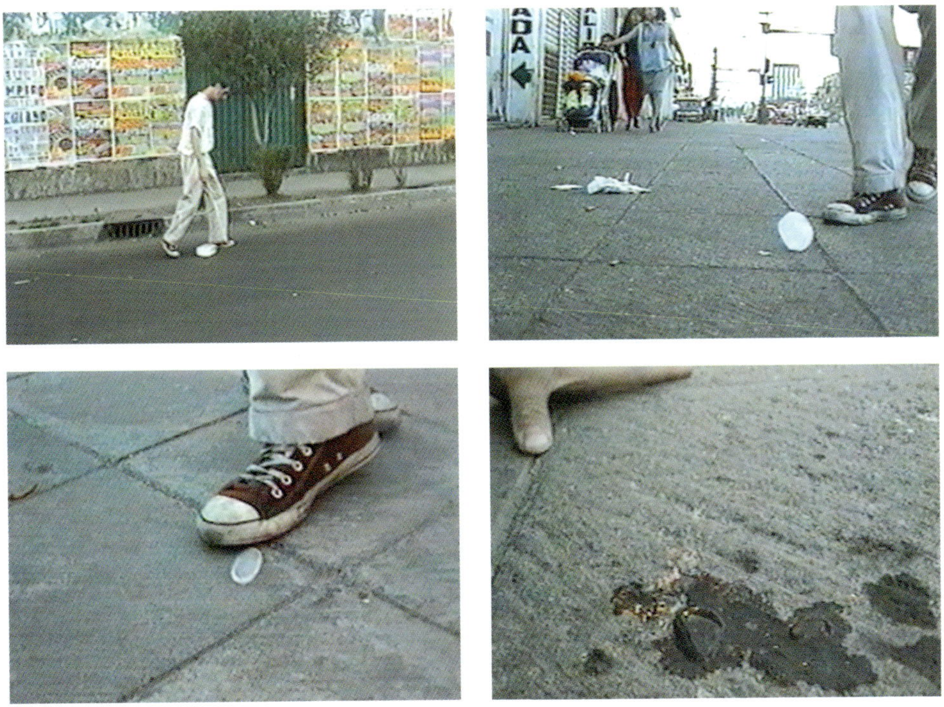

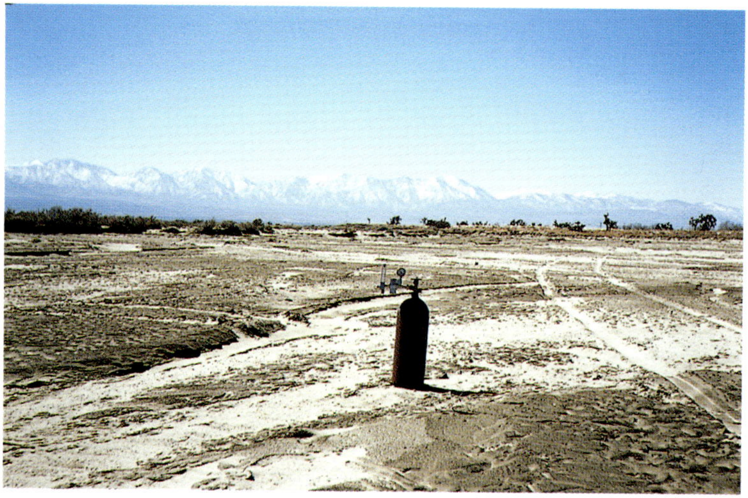

opposite:
Inert Gas Series
Robert Barry
1969

below:
whirlpool
Ann Lislegaard

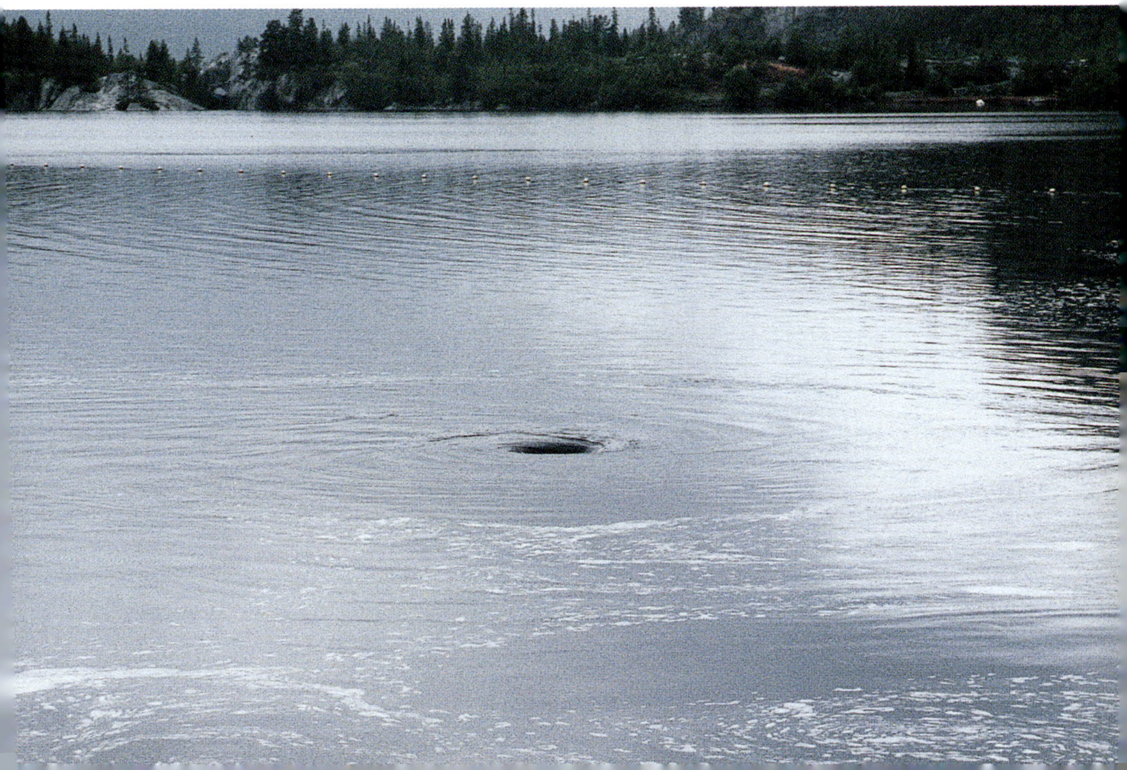

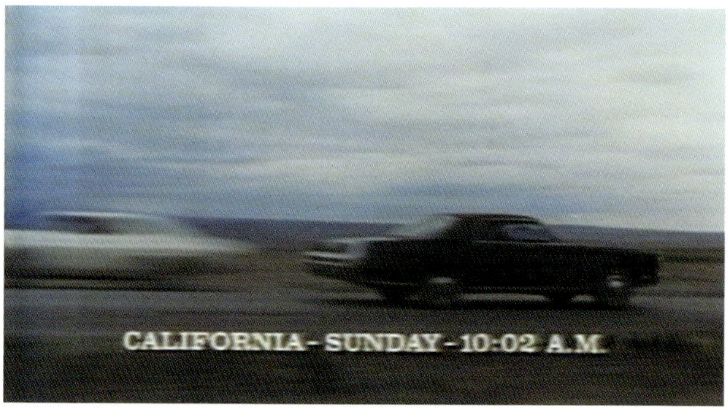

In *Vanishing Point*, a man makes a race-against-time road trip across the desert from Denver to San Francisco, chased by police. In the first few minutes of the film, we see the protagonist brake, turn and drive away from a barrier of bulldozers and pass another car. The narrative which then unfolds in cinematic 'real time' leads us to assume we are watching the events of his entire trip pass.

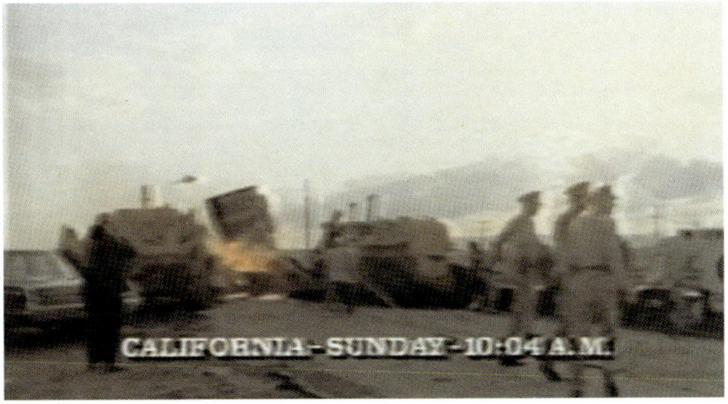

But towards the close of the film, we see the man's drive towards the police barrier repeated frame for frame – except this time he doesn't turn round, but accelerates and deliberately crashes into the bulldozers. A time-index caption fades up over the crash to indicate that only two minutes have in fact passed since the events shown at the start of the film.

The man drove seamlessly 'back' into the narrative as he turned, so there was no conventional break between past and present. We have not been watching images in flashback – time is shown to have looped back on itself – but images that do not seem to have existed at all.

Vanishing Point director Richard C Sarafian (1971)

Roadside Picnic
Arkady and Boris Strugatsky

1. REDRICK SCHUART,
AGE 23, BACHELOR, LABORATORY ASSISTANT AT THE HARMONT BRANCH OF THE INTERNATIONAL INSTITUTE FOR EXTRATERRESTRIAL CULTURES

... I was just standing there, holding up the wall, my work all done and a cigarette in my hand. I was dying for a smoke – it was two hours since I'd had one, and he was still puttering around with his stuff. He had loaded, locked, and sealed one safe and was loading up the other one – taking the empties from the transporter, examining each one from every angle (and they're heavy little bastards, by the way, fifteen pounds each), and carefully replacing them on the shelf.

He had been struggling with those empties forever, and the way I see it, without any benefit to humanity or himself. In his shoes, I would have said screw it long ago and gone to work on something else for the same money. Of course, on the other hand, if you think about it, an empty really is something mysterious and maybe even incomprehensible. I've handled quite a few of them, but I'm still surprised every time I see one. They're just two copper disks the size of a saucer, about a quarter inch thick, with a space of a foot and a half between them. There's nothing else. I mean absolutely nothing, just empty space. You can stick your hand in them, or even your head, if you're so knocked out by the whole thing – just emptiness and more emptiness, thin air. And for all that, of course, there is some force between them, as I understand it, because you can't press them together, and no-one's been able to pull them apart, either.

No, friends, it's hard to describe them to someone who hasn't seen them. They're too simple, especially when you look close and finally believe your eyes. It's like trying to describe a glass to someone: you end up wriggling your fingers and cursing in frustration. OK, let's say you've got it, and those of you who haven't get hold of a copy of the institute's Reports – every issue has an article on the empties with photos.

extracted from *Roadside Picnic*

opposite:
Wested Interchange (detail 4)
Sophy Rickett
1999

The Aesthetics of Disappearance
Paul Virilio

The lapse occurs frequently at breakfast and the cup dropped and overturned on the table is its well-known consequence. The absence lasts a few seconds; its beginning and its end are sudden. The senses function, but are nevertheless closed to external impressions. The return being just as sudden as the departure, the arrested word and action are picked up again where they have been interrupted. Conscious time comes together again automatically, forming a continuous time without apparent breaks. For these absences, which can be quite numerous – hundreds every day most often pass completely unnoticed by others around – we'll be using the word 'picnolepsy' (from the Greek, *picnos*: frequent). However, for the picnoleptic, nothing really has happened, the missing time never existed. At each crisis, without realising it, a little of his or her life simply escaped.

Children are the most frequent victims, and the situation of the young picnoleptic quickly becomes intolerable. People want to persuade him of the existence of events that he has not seen, though they effectively happened in his presence; and as he can't be made to believe in them he's considered a half-wit and convicted of lies and dissimulation. Secretly bewildered and tormented by the demands of those near him, in order to find information he needs constantly to stretch the limits of his memory. When we place a bouquet under the eyes of the young picnoleptic and we ask him to draw it, he draws not only the bouquet but also the person who is supposed to have placed it in the vase, and even the field of flowers where it was possibly gathered. There is a tendency to patch up sequences, readjusting their contours to make equivalents out of what the picnoleptic has seen and what he has not been able to see, what he remembers and what, evidently, he cannot remember and that it is necessary to invent, to recreate, in order to lend verisimilitude to his discursus. Later, the young picnoleptic will himself be inclined to doubt the knowledge and concordant evidence of those around him; everything certain will become suspect. He'll be inclined to believe (like Sextus Empiricus) that nothing really exists; that even if there is existence, it cannot be described; and that even if it could be described, it could certainly not be communicated or explained to others.

extracted from *The Aesthetics of Disappearance*

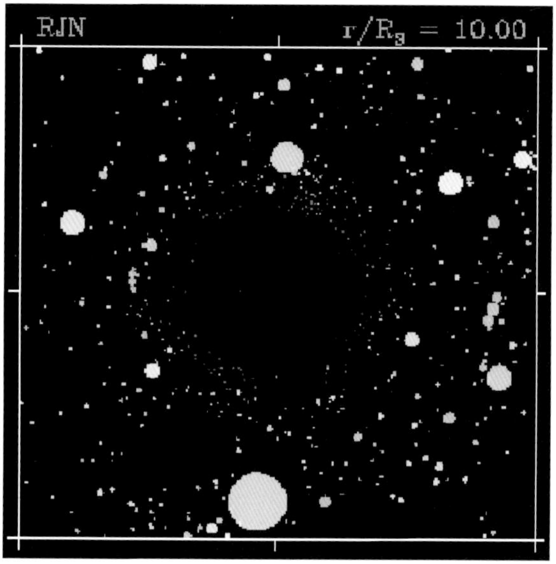
RJN
r/R₃ = 10.00

Black Holes
Isaac Asimov

Of all the odd creatures in the astronomical zoo, the 'black hole' is the oddest. To understand it, concentrate on gravity.

Every piece of matter produces a gravitational field. The larger the piece, the larger the field. What's more, the field grows more intense the closer you move to its centre. If a large object is squeezed into a smaller volume, its surface is nearer its centre and the gravitational pull on that surface is stronger.

Anything on the surface of a large body is in the grip of its gravity, and in order to escape it must move more rapidly. If it moves rapidly enough, then even though gravitational pull slows it down continually it can move sufficiently far away from the body so that the gravitational pull, weakened by distance, can never quite slow its motion to zero.

The minimum speed required for this is the 'escape velocity'. From the surface of the earth, the escape velocity is 7.0 miles per second. From Jupiter, which is larger, the escape velocity is 37.6 miles per second. From the sun, which is still larger, the escape velocity is 383.4 miles per second.

Imagine all the matter of the sun (which is a ball of hot gas 864,000 miles across) compressed tightly together. Imagine it compressed so tightly that its atoms smash and it becomes a ball of atomic nuclei and loose electrons, 30,000 miles across. The sun would then be a 'white dwarf'. Its surface would be nearer its centre, the gravitational pull on that surface would be stronger, and escape velocity would now be 2,100 miles per second.

Compress the sun still more to the point where the electrons melt into the nuclei. There would then be nothing left but tiny neutrons, and they will move together till they touch. The sun would then be only 9 miles across, and it would be a 'neutron star'. Escape velocity

opposite:
Black Hole, from a distance of 42.0km

would be 120,000 miles per second.

Few things material could get away from a neutron star, but light could, of course, since light moves at 186,282 miles per second.

Imagine the sun shrinking past the neutron-star stage, with the neutrons smashing and collapsing. By the time the sun is 3.6 miles across, escape velocity has passed the speed of light, and light can no longer escape. Since nothing can go faster than light, *nothing* can escape.

Into such a shrunken sun anything might fall, but nothing can come out. It would be like an endlessly deep hole in space. Since not even light can come out, it is utterly dark – it is a 'black hole'.

In 1939, J Robert Oppenheimer first worked out the nature of black holes in the light of the laws of modern physics, and ever since astronomers have wondered if black holes exist in fact as well as in theory.

How would they form? Stars would collapse under their own enormous gravity were it not for the enormous heat they develop, which keeps them expanded. The heat is formed by the fusion of hydrogen nuclei, however, and when the hydrogen is used up the star collapses.

A star like our sun will eventually collapse fairly quietly to a white dwarf. A more massive star will explode before it collapses, losing some of its mass in the process. If the portion that survives the explosion and collapses is more than 1.4 times the mass of the sun, it will surely collapse into a neutron star. If it is more than 3.2 times the mass of the sun, it must collapse into a black hole.

Since there are indeed massive stars, some of them have collapsed by now and formed black holes. But how can we detect one? Black holes are only a few miles across after all, give off no radiation, and are trillions of miles away.

There's one way out. If matter falls into a black hole, it gives off X-rays in the process. If a black hole is collecting a great deal of matter, enough X-rays may be given off for us to detect them.

Suppose two massive stars are circling each other in close proximity. One explodes and collapses into a black hole. The two objects continue to circle each other, but as the second stage star approaches explosion it expands. As it expands, some of its matter spirals into the black hole, and there is an intense radiation of X-rays as a result.

In 1965, an X-ray source was discovered in the constellation Cygnus and was named 'Cygnus X-1'. Eventually, the source was pinpointed to the near neighbourhood of a dim star, HD-226868, which is only dim because it is 10,000 light-years away. Actually, it is a huge star, 30 times the mass of our sun.

That star is one of a pair and the two are circling each other once every 5.6 days. The X-rays are coming from the other star, the companion of HD-226868, it is possible to calculate that Cygnus X-1 is 5 to 8 times the mass of our sun.

A star of that mass should be visible if it is an ordinary star, but no telescope can detect any star on the spot where X-rays are emerging. Cygnus X-1 must be a collapsed star that is too small to see. Since Cygnus X-1 is at least 5 times as massive as our sun, it is too massive to be a white dwarf; too massive, even, to be a neutron star.

It can be nothing other than a black hole; the first to be discovered.

Do not hear

Horizont

...jer misao u svom kretanju nosi poruku kroza strukturu memorije, koja se pri tome pokazuje kao višedimenzionalna. Upravo ova postignuta inverzija, smanjivanje dimenzija stvarnog objekta, tj. aktiviranja dimenzija naše memorije, rezultat je redukcije...

From David Hunter to Zero All is God

Charles Esche

It was only a fictional proposition, I thought.

The 'plane without a surface' first appeared in a short story by Ian McEwan entitled 'Solid Geometry'; a tale published in his collection *First Love, Last Rites* in 1975. As fiction it was worthy enough, but it was hardly to be taken seriously as a scientific document. In fact, like so many other stories, it might have simply disappeared from my consciousness, stored irretrievably amongst the rest of a teenager's pulp reading. But for some reason it caught a hold of a neural path in my brain and, as such things often do, provoked my natural nervous impulse to worry an idea to death and finally, to take it off the page and into my world.

The simple facts are these. An unknown Edinburgh mathematician called David Hunter turns up at a Viennese symposium in 1870 with a practical demonstration of zero dimensionality, a notion which undermines our whole canon of physical laws and forces one to redefine one's place in Nature's scheme. His demonstration involved folding a carefully-cut piece of paper up into itself until it vanished into nothingness. This much, I now believe, is true, not the fiction presented in 'Solid Geometry'; though whether Hunter subsequently used his own body as the subject and disappeared into thin air is not recorded in the surviving texts. Unquestionably, however, both Hunter and his discovery vanish from the records until McEwan picks up a corrupted version of the incident and uses it as a rather overblown vehicle for a tale of English marital boredom.

I should not be ungrateful however, because McEwan's discovery alerted me to the possibility of the zero dimension and the idea that, as it says in his text, dimensionality is a function of consciousness. Once awoken, such a thought is impossible to put back to sleep. Like the conspiracy theories spawned by many contemporary mysteries, investigating the plane without a surface seemed suddenly to reveal a whole arcane history of nothingness, as well as a cell of converts enlightened as to its existence and power.

To start with, as a young art historian, I picked up some strange, half-felt resonances from Robert Smithson and his descriptions of the cosmos in the planetarium:

> The planetarium becomes the same size as the universe; which it is. Perplexed, dizzied, one encounters here a cosmic nostalgia... Enormous lengths of time are compressed into the room. Light-years pass in minutes. Life so extended becomes negligible.[1]

Time and space stretched to infinity or reduced to zero. Things collapsed in on themselves. Not only is the measure of a human life held up to ridicule, but the passing of time itself becomes a measure of space rather than change. Movement is too short to be significant, but instead, time takes on the role of index to its own reality. Isn't this exactly what the plane without a surface proposes: that time, space and zero are one, and all there is?

But if Smithson was aware of this phenomenon, what really happened in 1971? Certainly his light aircraft crashed while circling a proposed sight for a landwork, but would he have appreciated the irony of his flightpath, folding in on itself, removing more and more space from his internal trajectory? Or, if we accept the reasonable proposition that his death was an accident, than we cannot deny the reality of the Spiral Jetty. What happens when a person runs out to the centre, as Smithson himself does at the end of the documentary film? Where does he, and any traveller on the jetty, go? A simple return to where he started seems such an un-Smithsonian solution; he was interested in permanent transformations, perhaps ultimately of himself.

As my investigation deepened, Smithson acted both as a gateway and as a kind of talisman to accompany a journey into the dimensions of nothingness. If the Spiral Jetty became a kind of Cape Canaveral for this mission, then the concept of zero dimensionality offered the co-ordinates, and mathematical analysis provided the power.

Mathematicians frequently deal with spaces that have dimensions much larger than three – sometimes hundreds. But there appears to be something mathematically unique about four-dimensional space.

> Mathematicians are normally cautious and meticulous individuals, but when they describe the results of their studies of four-dimensional space, they are apt to apply adjectives like 'bizarre', 'strange', 'weird', and 'mysterious'. By combining ideas borrowed from theoretical physics with abstract notions from the field of topology, mathematicians are discovering that four-dimensional space – a realm just a short step beyond our own similar, three-dimensional world – has mathematical properties quite unlike those characterising space in any other dimension.[2]

This may be because the fourth dimension 'wraps back around' on zero-dimensionality (represented by the mathematical 'point'). We normally picture dimensions in a way that mislead us when we think of them as separate objects that are independent of each other, like limbs growing from a tree trunk. Scientist Arthur Young conceives of their relationship in a rather different way. He models the relationship between dimensions on the relationship between the 'time derivatives' in calculus. The relationship between the dimensions, in other words, is similar to the relationship between 'distance' (the first dimension), 'velocity' (the second dimension), and 'acceleration' (the third dimension) – where change in distance with respect to time is velocity, and change with respect to time is acceleration. The 'fourth dimension' (which would be equivalent to 'change in acceleration with respect to time'), argues Young, brings us full-circle back to the conceptual equivalent of distance or 'position' – in a way that suggests that the reality in which we live as humans has a 'liminocentric structure'.

When 'zero-dimensionality' (which is ignored by Young) is taken into consideration, the fourth dimension might be thought of as wrapping back not on the first dimension, but on the starting place for the entire sequence: emptiness (the mathematical point, as opposed to the line which we use to represent distance). We could therefore say that the dimensions of human reality are hierarchically nested, but in a non-linear (or 'circular') fashion, with the top-most level of the hierarchy wrapping back round on the bottom-most.

Young's hypothesis might explain why the fourth dimension is literally missing in our world, as this dimension would simply appear to us as zero-dimensionality: nothingness. The description also seems to parallel Jung's notion of the 'missing fourth', which it enriches by linking it to scientific speculations about the fundamental structure of reality and related philosophical and pyschological speculations about the fundamental structure of consciousness.

If the fourth dimension does indeed wrap around onto the zero-dimension, the joining would seem to occur somewhere between the third and fourth dimension. In 'fractal geometry' (which we might call the 'geometry of liminocentric structures') one is permitted fractional dimensions. You can have objects that are 2-dimensional, and 3-dimensional; but you can also have objects that are 1.5-dimensional, or 2.73-dimensional. Is it possible that the turning point, the place where the dimensional wrapping occurs, is at the fractional dimension equal to 'pi'? *Pi* was at one time approximated as 22.7ths (or 3 1/7, which equals 3.142857). If dimensions have this kind of chinese-box relationship with each other, then 3 1/7 turnings of the 'wheel' (or 'circumnabulations' of the 'mandala') might take us not only into the centre, but also shoot us full-circle back out to our starting point at the periphery. The spiral returns within this sub-species of psycho-Buddhist mathematics as though anticipating not only Smithson's work, but the origin of the 1870 lecture and McEwan's description of David Hunter's body folding in on itself. McEwan has Hunter demonstrate his proposal for the plane without a surface on himself:

> Hunter strode through the crowd to a couch which stood along one of the walls, and while he settled himself upon it he told the mystified Goodman that when he returned to England he should take with him Hunter's papers and keep them there until he came to collect them. When the mathematicians had gathered round the couch Hunter rolled on to his stomach and clasped his hands behind his back in a strange posture to fashion a hoop with his arms. He asked Goodman to hold his arms in that position for him, and rolled onto his side where he began a number of strenuous jerking movements which enabled him to pass one of his feet through the hoop. He asked his assistant to turn him on his side, where he performed the same movements again and succeeded in passing his other foot between his arms, and at the same time bent his trunk in such a way that his head was able to pass through the hoop in the opposite direction to his feet. With the help of his assistant he began to pass his leg and head past each other through the hoop made by his arms. It was then that the distinguished assembly vented, as one man, a single yelp of utter incredulity. Hunter was beginning to disappear, and now, as his legs and head passed through his arms with greater facility, seemed even to be

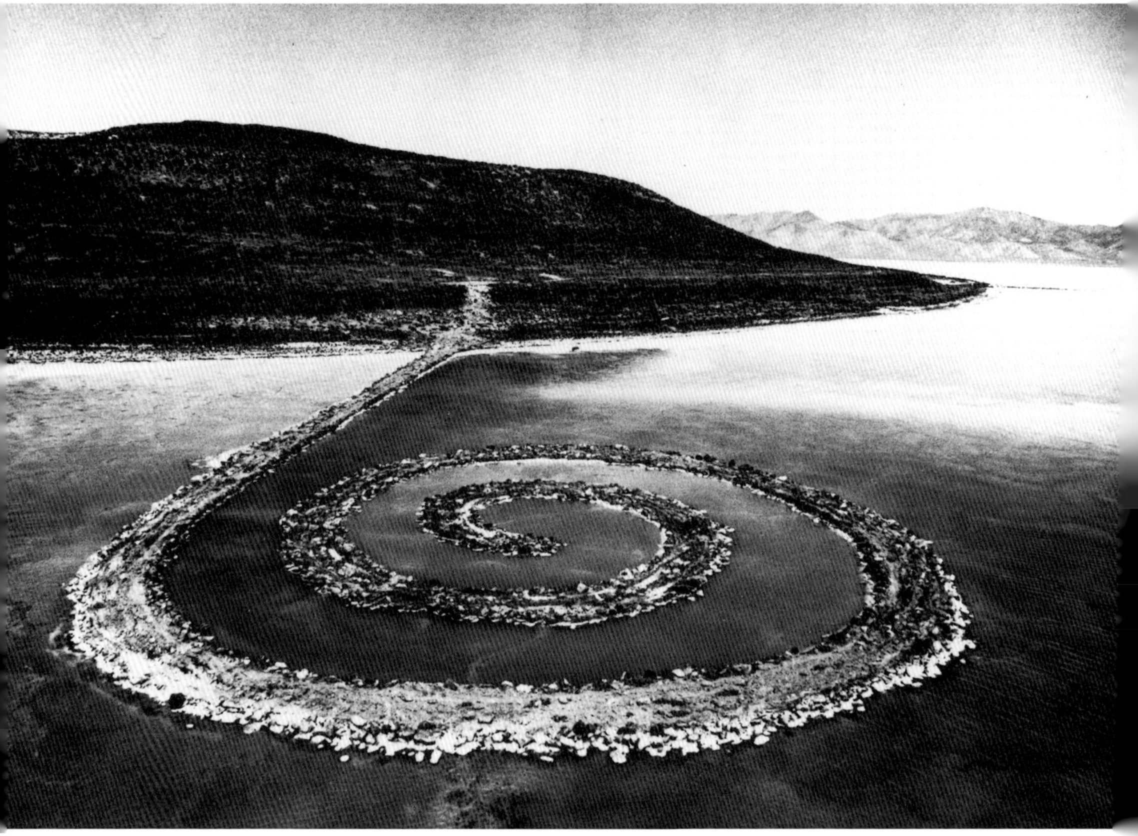

Spiral Jetty
Robert Smithson
1970

> drawn through by some invisible power, he was almost gone. And now he was gone, quite gone, and nothing remained.[3]

If this incident is true, then presumably Hunter knew into what dimension or time he would dissolve. He even goes so far as to assure his unwilling assistant Goodman to retain his papers until he collected them. Sadly, McEwan doesn't explore the disappearance further. However, arcane accounts from the sixteenth century suggest one theosophical explanation.

In the 1500s, two Christ apostles in the Order of Sion experimented with Psilocyban mushrooms, in an attempt to create the Eucharist (this Manna Mushroom, appearing like the holy grail, being one of the ancient mystifications added by the Amen priests, to replace the genuine harmine Pinoline DMT Soma/Akashia sources, which the pineal gland produces as the third eye). The spirit medium Falconelli contacted them (Nicholas Flammel and his wife), and taught them the true Agape Sacrament. They too superconducted and disappeared into the Word, remanifesting to give clues here and there.

At a recent topological symposium at the Economical University in Prague, two mathematicians, G F Ondersteegen and D E Tymchatkayn, proposed the existence not only of zero dimensions, but also of almost-zero dimensions that provide a convenient viewpoint on the study of totally disconnected (at most) one-dimensional spaces.

The paper, in an odd English translation from Belarussian, sought to demonstrate:

> ...how disregarding the philosophical approach at solving physics problems, on the basis of a concrete example of dimensionality establishment, leads to serious consequences, and to what extent.
> A transformation of the dimensionalities of physical quantities, for both electric as well as magnetic fields with fractional powers of CGS units (that are the basis for SI units) into dimensionalities with integer powers of the units, gets at present exclusively important meaning, especially, after the disaster at Chernobyl's atomic station. An understanding of the nature of the electric charge and electromagnetic field and more profound penetration in the essence of atom structure depends on solving this problem, that has to promote in the nearest future an atomic technology's perfecting.

Numerous attempts in the first half of the twentieth century to solve the dimensionality problem by physics itself have met with failure. The reason is that the problem lies on the boundary of philosophy and physics and can be solved only on the basis of philosophic-physical analysis. We examine this problem using our solutions.

Their solutions suggested the breakdown of geometric analysis of dimensions and its replacement with a fundamental acceptance of the zero dimension as the controlling and accessible foundation of all subsequent subjectivities using the following proof:

Let I be an ideal of the polynomial ring P = K [x_1, …, x_n]. Let X be the set { x_1, …, x_n } of variables of P. A subset of U of X is called independent modulo I if I intersect K[U] = emptyset. A subset of U of X is called maximally independent modulo I if U is independent modulo I, and no proper superset of U is independent modulo I. The dimension of I is defined to be the maximum of the cardinalities of all the independent sets modulo I. Note that the definition given above of zero-dimensionality (as the case when the quotient of P by I has finite dimension as a vector space over the coefficient field) coincides with the definition of zero-dimensionality as dimension 0.

If Hunter, Smithson, McEwan and others have known this for the last 130 years, how has it not penetrated conventional art and science? One plausible explanation could be their own disappearance into the Word followed by instant and significant suppression of their discoveries. Only in the conspiracy-rich world of minor cults, religious fanatics and Hindu-Buddhist-Christian-Kabbalic miscegenations does some of this imagined secret find expression.

Break down the word 'GOD' to smaller units, i.e. 'G' 'O' 'D', and then witness what is ascribed to those letters? G is used in G-Force, or Gravity; O is used for null, nil, or 0 (zer0); D is used for dimension, such as 3-D, 4-D. Hence, by breaking down a mystical word to smaller units, we came up with Gravity Zero Dimension (Gravity at zero dimensionality, is beyond universal constructs). Electrogravity, is zero-point gravity, and this is the Vortexjah, it is infinite speed united with all possible speeds at all times and spaces, through its marriage with zero speed.

When we understand this, we can no longer be run by a system of geometry, but rather by the perfect All is God Vortexjah Unit that is

Us perfectly. Hence, any heaven Light Station or God Source is a 'Lord of the Flame' paradigm. Lucifire-LuciPHire-Lucifer is the Lord of the Flame the second Logos, as the Lux-I-Fire. Light requires sacrifice to burn, this requires hierarchy. Flame is spiral, which is spin, which is the geometry of Limitation. Let us be Self Born. Let us Self create our Soul Implants from our Infinite and Zero All Is God Vortexijah Unity Units. Remember this viewpoint, as some foundation may shatter ahead.

see page 200 for footnotes

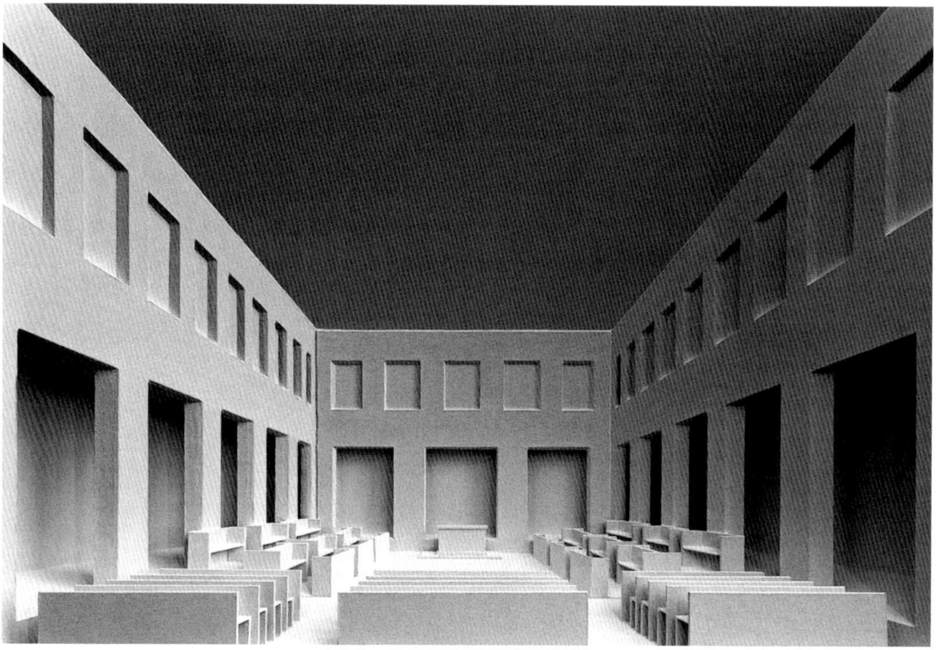

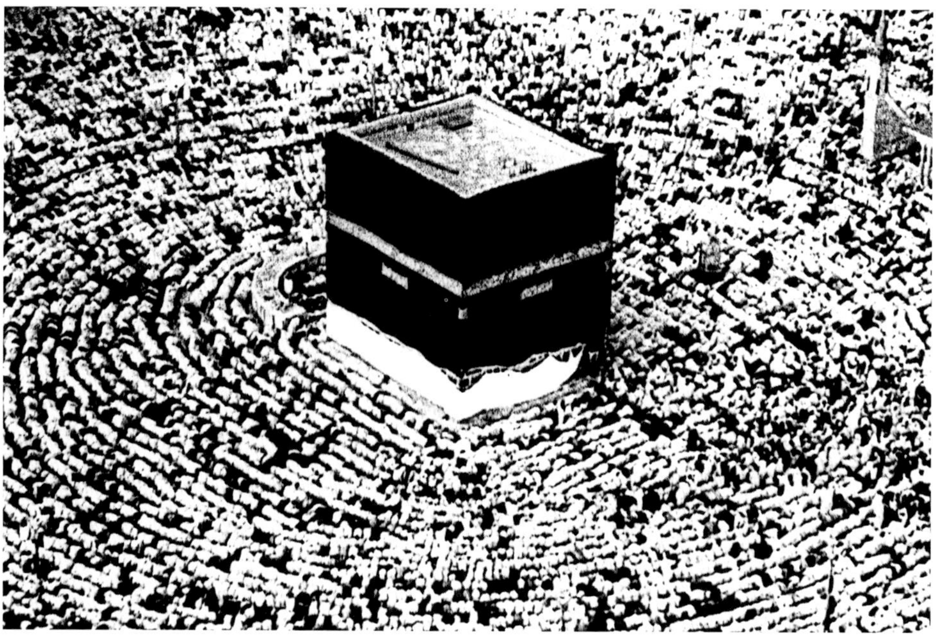

Nothing: Space for Oblivion

If architecture at its most elementary represents an attempt to reconcile the apparent endlessness of nature, by defining a personal or social space within the natural space of the wider world, religious architecture seeks to emphasise a personal/social space within the absolute space of oblivion.

The geometry of the religious building is predicated on the assumption of a mythic geometry which orders events beyond the building's point of focus – beyond the Altar, Ark, or *Ka'ba* – beyond this world.

The temporal reality of this geometry is a structure in which the spiritual dimensions of a community take physical form in an emblematic act of enclosure, where belief or a moment of intent is retained symbolically – in the face of oblivion.

Langlands & Bell, 2000

al-hayrah – a constant circular movement
around a point mentally incomprehensible.
Ibn 'Arabi (1165–1240)

3 No-Plays

No-Play No1

This is a play nobody must come and see. That is, the not-coming of anyone makes the play. Together with the very extensive advertising of the spectacle through newspapers, radio, TV, private invitations, etc...
No one must be told not to come.
No one should be told that he really shouldn't come.
No one must be prevented from coming in any way whatsoever!!!
But nobody must come, or there is no play.
That is, if the spectators come, there is no play. And if no spectators come, there is no play either... I mean, one way or the other there is a play, but it is a No-Play.

No-Play No2

In this No-Play, time/space is of the essence. It consists of a performance during which no spectator becomes older. If the spectators become older from the time they come to the performance to the time they leave it, then there is no play. That is to say, there is a play, but it is a No-Play.

Robert Filliou, 1964

Never believe an artist who says their work is about nothing: the culture consumer's fear of the void
Pierre Bismuth

'Your paintings are like my films, they are about nothing... with precision.'
Michelangelo Antonioni to Mark Rothko (1962)

– 'Polyphemus, what dire affliction has come upon you to make you profane the night with clamour and rob us of our slumbers? [...] Is someone threatening death to yourself by craft or by violence?'
– 'Friends, it is Noman's craft and no violence that is threatening death to me.'
– 'If you are alone, then this is a malady sent by almighty Zeus, from which there is no escape.'
Homer, *The Odyssey* (trans. Walter Shewring)

One often has occasion to observe the remarkable degree to which the public simply accepts an artist's statement about a work of art and, in a way, maintains its trust in there being a faithful correspondence between the statement and the realisation; as if the statement was not a production in its own right with its own logic and motives but offered unmediated information about the way the work is to be perceived. And yet it must be allowed that a work may be motivated by circumstances that are alien to its definition, quite simply because this definition corresponds either to what the artist wants to show (as opposed to what can be seen in the work), or to the position that the artist wants us to adopt with regard to the work. To call into question the meaning or value of the statement would not, however, imply calling into question the artist's good faith or intelligence. It is not a matter of knowing whether the work is or is not what it is said to be, but of understanding the motives behind a choice of definition and being aware of the possible gap separating it from what it designates.

It's very simple. Art that claims to be about nothing, absence, silence, emptiness, vacuity, nothingness, ugliness, meaninglessness, uselessness, trivia, the negligible, the absurd, boredom… never is. We could even say that for the observer who is not taken in or deluded by the statement, such works produce precisely the opposite effect. How can it be that nothing is always something, and what is it that makes an artist want to attain this dimension of absence if, ultimately, they already know that the undertaking is vain, the project impossible? I am not going to try to analyse the ways of formally expressing nothingness here, or the strategies of formally incorporating nothingness in the actual making of an artwork. I would simply like to show that the use of this concept of nothingness, as applied to the artist's statement about the work, constitutes a strategy designed to dash our hopes as viewers.

But what are these hopes and on what are they based? More than ever, on our shared political and social context. Since art now speaks to an increasingly wide and, therefore, not necessarily educated audience, it cannot be presented on the basis of a shared artistic culture but must use values that are not specifically related to art and its history. These values are for the most part produced by an economic system based on production and consumption, on the belief in information and communication, on the need for events, tourism, distractions and signs of progress. Curiously, though, even the most disenchanted consumer may still harbour some credulity towards art. While he or she would be spontaneously sceptical towards the discourse surrounding consumer goods, they might well tend to believe an artist who vaunts the absence of aesthetic qualities in a blank canvas and to consider that there is indeed nothing here to be looked at. We are aware of the commercial impact of lies about quality when it comes to consumer goods, but we find it harder to understand why an artist might wish to devalue his of her own work. Why this publicity concerning the emptiness of the work if that was not really the case?

One of the answers put forward by maladroit upholders of an art based on negative values is to attempt to develop a discourse on the hidden qualities of nothingness. This presumptuous position makes the mistake of thinking that vacuity is a materially achievable quality and not just a concept. 'Nothingness' constitutes a strategy that enables an artist to free his or her activity from any form of social pressure. This nothingness defines the absence of qualities from a sarcastic viewpoint, referring to the idea of an economic system based on the daily production of artificial values. The idea of making nothing both marks a refusal to take part in the blindness of all the hype, and anticipates the viewer's value judgements and possible disappointment. The artist who claims that their work is about nothing is doing nothing more than using the public language and judgmental values produced by this system. A work on nothingness, assuming it could exist, would in a sense be the essence of aesthetic production as it is habitually seen from a bourgeois perspective.

If viewers are not aware that this 'nothing' is merely a trick of language embodying a critical attitude towards the social system and expectations of art, it is because they never think of assessing the discrepancy between the definition of the work and its physical reality – in other words, of analysing the way in which it is implemented and made and presented. If viewers do not undertake this task, that is because in most cases they position themselves as cultural consumers, outside the creative process, whereas in fact they should always consider themselves as the potential creator of the work. Each one of us creates at each moment of the day in the way we live and understand reality. The artist's sole quality is to be aware of this and to make it manifest in the context of art and in accordance with the artistic conventions to which he or she subscribes. Artists are artists only because they define themselves as such and, by using the strategy of nothingness, they confirm the old idea that the artwork is made by those who look at it. In art, 'nothing' exists only for those who are ready to believe in it.

Translated by C Penwarden

opposite:
Total Eclipse
12 August 1999

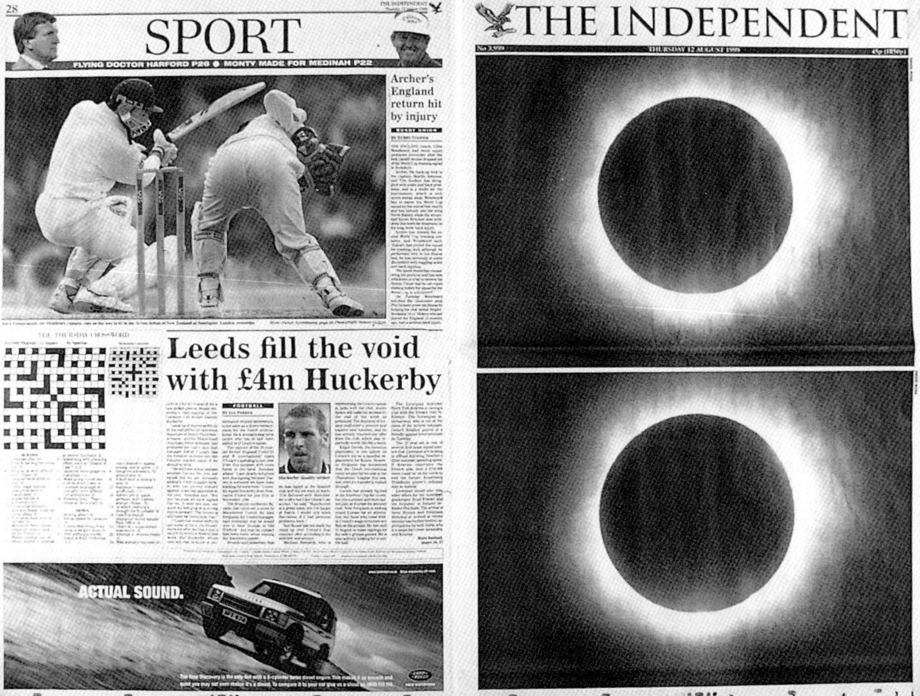

28

THE INDEPENDENT

SPORT

FLYING DOCTOR HARFORD P26 ● MONTY MADE FOR MEDINAH P22

Archer's England return hit by injury

RUGBY UNION

THE THURSDAY CROSSWORD

Leeds fill the void with £4m Huckerby

FOOTBALL

THE INDEPENDENT

No 3,999 THURSDAY 12 AUGUST 1999 45p (IR50p)

How the World Was Saved
Stanislaw Lem

One day Trurl the constructor put together a machine that could create anything starting with n. When it was ready, he tried it out, ordering it to make needles, then nankeens and negligees, which it did, then nail the lot to narghiles filled with nepenthe and numerous other narcotics. The machine carried out his instructions to the letter. Still not completely sure of its ability, he had it produce, one after the other, nimbuses, noodles, nuclei, neutrons, naphtha, noses, nymphs, naiads, and natrium. This last it could not do, and Trurl, considerably irritated, demanded an explanation.

'Never heard of it,' said the machine.

'What? But it's only sodium. You know, the metal, the element...'

'Sodium starts with an s, and I work in n.'

'But in Latin it's natrium.'

'Look, old boy,' said the machine, 'if I could do everything starting with n in every possible language, I'd be a Machine That Could Do Everything in the Whole Alphabet, since any item that you care to mention undoubtedly starts with n in one foreign language or another. It's not that easy. I can't go beyond what you programmed. So no sodium.'

'Very well,' said Trurl and ordered it to make Night, which it made at once – small perhaps, but perfectly nocturnal. Only then did Trurl invite over his friend Klapaucius the constructor, and introduced him to the machine, praising its extraordinary skill at such length, that Klapaucius grew annoyed and inquired whether he too might not test the machine.

'Be my guest,' said Trurl. 'But is has to start with n.'

'N?' said Klapaucius. 'All right, let it make Nature.'

The machine whined, and in a trice Trurl's front yard was packed with naturalists. They argued, each publishing heavy volumes, which the others tore to pieces; in the distance one could see flaming pyres, on which martyrs to Nature were sizzling; there was thunder, and strange mushroom-shaped columns of smoke rose up; everyone talked at once, no-one listened, and there were all sorts of memoranda, appeals, subpoenas and other documents, while off to the side sat a few old men, feverishly scribbling on scraps of paper.

'Not bad, eh?' said Trurl with pride. 'Nature to a T, admit it!'

But Klapaucius wasn't satisfied.

'What, that mob? Surely you're not going to tell me that's Nature?'

'Then give the machine something else,' snapped Trurl. 'Whatever you like.' For a moment Klapaucius was at a loss for what to ask. But after a little thought he declared that he would put two more tasks to the machine; if it could fulfil them, he would admit that it was all Trurl said it was. Trurl agreed to this, whereupon Klapaucius requested Negative.

'Negative?!' cried Trurl. 'What on earth is Negative?'

'The opposite of positive, of course,' Klapaucius coolly replied. 'Negative attitudes, the negative of a picture, for example. Now don't try to pretend you never heard of Negative. All right machine, get to work!'

The machine however, had already begun. First it manufactured antiprotons, then antielectrons, antineutrons, antineutrinos, and laboured on, until from out of all this antimatter an antiworld took shape, glowing like a ghostly cloud above their heads.

'H'm,' muttered Klapaucius, displeased. 'That's supposed to be Negative? Well... let's say it is, for the sake of peace. ... But now here's the third command: Machine, do Nothing!'

The machine sat still. Klapaucius rubbed his hands in triumph, but Trurl said:

'Well, what did you expect? You asked for it to do nothing, and it's doing nothing.'

'Nothing is nothing!'

'Come, come. It was supposed to do Nothing, but it hasn't done anything, and therefore I've won. For Nothing, my dear and clever colleague, is not your run-of-the-mill nothing, the result of idleness and inactivity, but dynamic, aggressive Nothingness, that is to say, perfect, unique, ubiquitous, in other words Nonexistence, ultimate and supreme, in its very own nonperson!'

'You're confusing the machine!' cried Trurl. But suddenly its metallic voice rang out:

'Really, how can you two bicker at a time like this? Oh yes, I know what Nothing is, and Nothingness, Nonexistence, Nonentity, Negation, Nullity and Nihility, since all these come under the heading of n, n as in Nil. Look then upon your world for the last time, gentlemen! Soon it shall no longer be...'

The constructors froze, forgetting their quarrel, for the machine was in actual fact doing Nothing, and it did it in this fashion: one by one, various things were removed from the world, and the things, thus removed, ceased to exist, as it they had never been. The machine had already disposed of nolars, nightzebs, nocs, necs, nallyrakers, neotremes and nonmalrigers. At moments, though, it seemed that instead of reducing, diminishing and subtracting, the machine was increasing, enhancing and adding, since it liquidated, in turn: nonconformists, nonentities, nonsense, nonsupport, nearsightedness, narrowmindedness, naughtiness, neglect, nausea, necrophilia and nepotism. But after a while the world very definitely began to thin out around Trurl and Klapaucius.

'Omigosh!' said Trurl. 'If only nothing bad comes out of all this...'

'Don't worry,' said Klapaucius. 'You can see it's not producing Universal Nothingness, but only causing the absence of whatever starts with n. Which is really nothing in the way of nothing, and nothing is what your machine, dear Trurl is worth!'

'Do not be deceived,' replied the machine. 'I've begun, it's true, with everything in n, but only out of familiarity. To create however is one thing, to destroy, another thing entirely. I can blot out the world for the simple reason that I'm able to do anything and everything – and everything means everything – in n, and consequently, Nothingness is child's play for me. In less than a minute now you will cease to have existence, along with everything else, so tell me now, Klapaucius, and quickly, that I am really and truly everything I was programmed to be, before it is too late.'

'But –' Klapaucius was about to protest, but noticed, just then, that a number of things were indeed disappearing, and not merely those that started with n. The constructors were no longer surrounded by the gruncheons, the targalisks, the shupops, the calinatifacts, the thists, worches and pritons.

'Stop! I take it all back! Desist! Whoa! Don't do Nothing!!' screamed Klapaucius. But before the machine could come to a full stop, all the brashations, plusters, laries and zits had vanished away. Now the machine stood motionless. The world was a dreadful sight. The sky had particularly suffered: there were only a few, isolated points of light in the heavens – no trace of the glorious worches and zits that had, till now, graced the horizon!

'Great Gauss!' cried Klapaucius. 'And where are the gruncheons? Where my dear, favourite pritons? Where now the gentle zits?!'

'They no longer are, nor ever will exist again,' the machine said calmly. 'I executed, or rather only began to execute, your order...'

'I tell you to do Nothing, and you... you...'

'Klapaucius, don't pretend to be a greater idiot than you are,' said the machine. 'Had I made Nothing outright, in one fell swoop, everything would have ceased to exist, and that includes Trurl, the sky, the Universe, and you – and even myself. In which case who could say and to whom could it be said that the order was carried out and I am an efficient and capable machine? And if no-one could say it to no-one, in what way then could I, who also would not be, be vindicated?'

'Yes, fine, let's drop the subject,' said Klapaucius. 'I have nothing more to ask of you, only please, dear machine, please return the zits, for without them life loses all its charm...'

'But I can't, they're in z,' said the machine. 'Of course, I can restore nonsense, narrowmindedness, nausea, necrophilia, neuralgia, nefariousness and noxiousness. As for the other letters, however, I can't help you.'

'I want my zits!' bellowed Klapaucius.

'Sorry, no zits,' said the machine.'Take a good look at this world, how riddled it is with huge, gaping holes, how full of Nothingness, the Nothingness that fills the bottomless void between the stars, how everything about us has become lined with it, how it darkly lurks behind each shred of matter. This your work, envious one! And I hardly think the future generations will bless you for it...'

'Perhaps... they won't find out, perhaps they won't notice,' groaned the pale Klapaucius, gazing up incredulously at the black emptiness of space and not daring to look his colleague, Trurl, in the eye. Leaving him beside the machine that could do everything in n, Klapaucius skulked home – and to this day the world has remained honey-combed with nothingness, exactly as it was when halted in the course of its liquidation. And as all subsequent attempts to build a machine on any other letter met with failure, it is to be feared that never again will we have such marvellous phenomena as the worches and the zits – no, never again.

You are all indicted; stand up! Stand up as you would for the Marseillaise or God Save the King....

Dada alone does not smell: it is nothing, nothing, nothing.

It is like your hopes: nothing.
like your paradise: nothing.
like your idols: nothing.
like your politicians: nothing.
like your heroes: nothing.
like your artists: nothing.
like your religions: nothing.

Hiss, shout, kick my teeth in, so what? I shall still tell you that you are half-wits. In three months my friends and I will be selling you our pictures for a few francs.

Manifeste cannibale dada by Francis Picabia, read at the Dada soirée at the Théâtre de la Maison de l'Oeuvre, Paris, 27 March 1920

Scientists get to the heart of the antimatter

Tim Radford
Science editor

European scientists have started making the ultimate hard-to-handle product — antimatter. Yesterday they turned on their new antiproton decelerator at Cern, the European particle laboratory in Geneva, and started the tricky business of manipulating a material that would destroy anything it touched.

Antimatter is matter in reverse. It is created in particle accelerators, but when it meets ordinary fabric, both matter and antimatter are annihilated in a colossal burst of energy.

Scientists at Cern see antimatter appear and disappear instantaneously during every second of their experiments. But they have seen only the equivalents of parts of atoms, rather than atoms themselves. Physicists have known about positrons (positively charged electrons) and antiprotons for decades. The proton is the positively charged bit at the heart of the atom; the electron is the light, negatively charged bit that balances it.

In 1996, scientists at Cern went further, making nine atoms of antihydrogen, which perished almost immediately. Antiparticles are born from experiments in an accelerator which takes matter almost to the speed of light. The new instrument, the 188m antiproton decelerator, gathers the antiprotons in bunches, slows them down, traps them in electromagnetic cages and slows them almost to a standstill. All this has to be done in a perfect vacuum. At this point, two groups of scientists plan to add positrons — used in brain scans— to the antiprotons to make antihydrogen. A third group are planning to use the helium atom as a kind of antiproton-catcher.

The antimatter will be made only in the tiniest trickles — all the antimatter made in Europe and the US in the last two decades would add up to less than a millionth of a gram. But once they have amassed their imprisoned anti-atoms, scientists can study their behaviour.

Space scientists have a direct interest: they calculate that even a small lump of antimatter — perhaps 20kg — could drive something the size of the Starship Enterprise around the galaxy. More directly, the experiment could begin to answer: why is the universe made of matter, rather than antimatter? All the evidence is that when matter condenses from energy, it does so in equal quantities of matter and antimatter. But unless there was slightly more matter than antimatter in the first moments of creation, the two should have destroyed each other.

"In this cosmic battleground, matter came out the winner and we are all here. But that defies the understanding of physics," said Neil Calder of Cern, yesterday. "Exactly the same amount of matter and antimatter is produced, so we shouldn't be here. But we are."

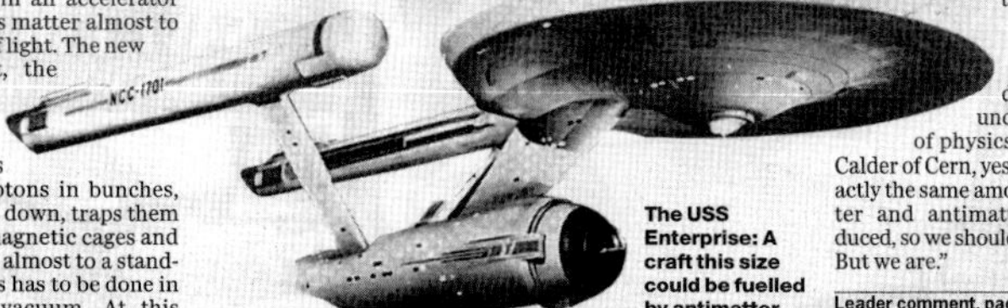

The USS Enterprise: A craft this size could be fuelled by antimatter

Leader comment, page 19

Some Void Thoughts on Museums
Robert Smithson

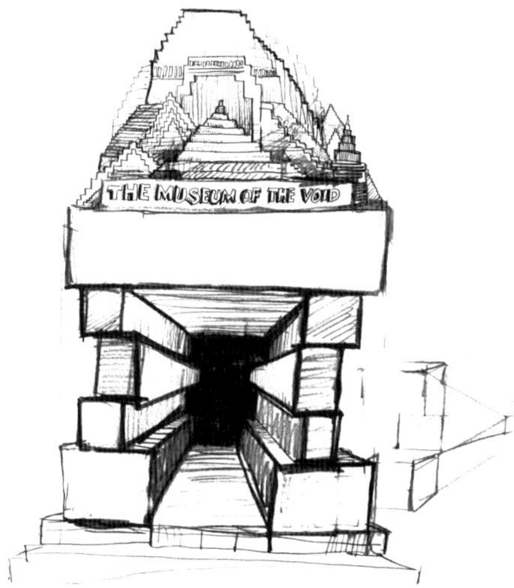

The Museum of the Void
Robert Smithson
1967

> Tomb furniture achieved apparently contradictory ends in discarding old things all the while retaining them, much as in our storage warehouses, and museum deposits, and antiquarian storerooms.
> George Kubler, *The Shape of Time: Remarks on the History of Things*

History is a facsimile of events held together by flimsy biographical information. Art history is less explosive than the rest of history, so it sinks faster into the pulverised regions of time. History is representational, while time is abstract; both of these artifices may be found in museums, where they span everybody's own vacancy. The museum undermines one's confidence in sense-data and erodes the impression of textures upon which our sensations exist. Memories of 'excitement' seem to promise something, but nothing is always the result. Those with exhausted memories will know the astonishment.

Visiting a museum is a matter of going from void to void. Hallways lead the viewer to things once called 'pictures' and 'statues'. Anachronisms hang and protrude from every angle. Themes without meaning press on the eye. Multifarious nothings permute into false windows (frames) that open up onto a verity of blanks. Stale images cancel one's perception and deviate one's motivation. Blind and senseless, one continues wandering around the remains of Europe, only to end in that massive deception 'the art history of the recent past.' Brain drain leads to eye drain, as one's sight defines emptiness by blankness. Sightings fall like heavy objects from one's eyes. Sight becomes devoid of perceptual falling out by calling it abstract. Abstraction is everybody's zero but nobody's nought. Museums are tombs, and it looks like everything is turning into a museum. Painting, sculpture and architecture are finished, but the art habit continues. Art settles into a stupendous inertia. Silence supplies the dominant chord. Bright colours conceal the abyss that holds the museum together. Every solid is a bit of clogged air or space. Things flatten and fade. The museum spreads its surfaces everywhere, and becomes an untitled collection of generalisations that immobilise the eye.

Ligne d'abandon
(sleeve for CD project)
Gabriel Orozco and
Manuel Rocha
1996

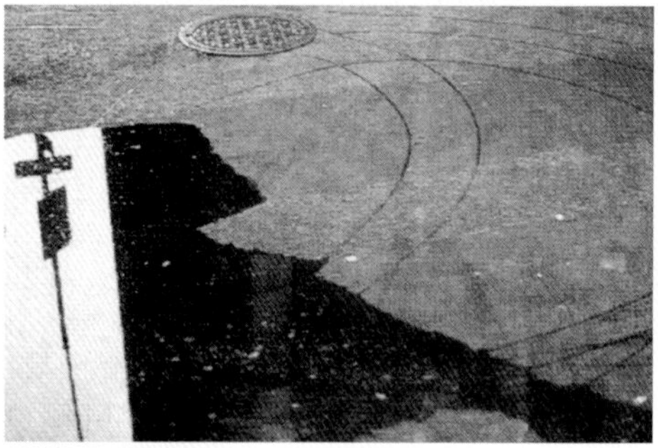

GABRIEL OROZCO "LA EXTENSION DEL REFLEJO"
NEW YORK 1992

Ligne d'abandon is a sound piece based on the noise generated by the screeching wheels of a car. We were intrigued by this noise and its relationship to a possible accident. The uncertainty about what can happen afterwards: the screeching noise generates a sort of feeling that could be related to void, suspended time or collapse.

We were also attracted by the characteristics of its source: the friction of the car wheel with the pavement, the rubber wheel grazing against a hard surface, being eroded and leaving its trace (related to Orozco's work *Piedra que cede* and *La extensión del Reflejo*) and the possibility to express this aurally. Moreover we chose this noise because of its intrinsic quality in terms of timbre: its high frequency, which is piercing and can also be anguishing.

We decided to extend the physical and metaphoric qualities of the screeching wheel's noise by manipulating it with a computer. By stretching and contracting it by different lengths with a "Phase Vocoder", and by multiplying it by itself (Convolution), the spectral characteristics were strengthened. The sound was then filtered to lighten the presence of high frequencies. From the original sound lasting 7 seconds, and the longest stretching lasting for 40 seconds, we chose 7 different transformations of various lengths that go from 40 seconds (the longest) to two seconds (the shortest).

We then structured the piece by using two series of time durations. One of the series consists of 5 sounds in decreasing order, the last one always being changed between three possibilities. The other series consist of 8 durations of silence in decreasing order, every silent duration being coupled with every sound. As a result, we have a process that starts with long sounds and silent durations being reduced, but since we have eight silent durations and only five sound durations, at one point the sounds start to get out of phase and they start to mix between them in an "accidental" way. When this mechanism comes to an end, it starts all over again with the 5 isolated sounds in decreasing time order. The whole process lasts for 30 minutes.

Having sounds getting out of phase with silent duration's, there are sometimes long moments when nothing is heard, and other moments when all sounds are mixed together. "Accident" and "Chance" generate their own orbit. On the other hand, the static qualities of the sound make the piece always stable and give it a sense of continuum, even if at certain moments there is a strange simultaneity of events. During the actual playing of the piece in a specific space (the piece is played continuously, so we advice you to activate the repeat function of youre CD player) the long periods of silence are relevant, since people can come in and out of the space without knowing at what point the piece is playing. However, ***Ligne d'abandon*** can also be listened linearly, from the beginning to the end, thanks to five isolated sounds that mark the beginning.

It could be interesting to mention that this sound work was developed in parallel to the process of making **La DS** , a Citroen DS spliced along in two parallel lines, removing the center space (62 cm.), and then assembled again, generating another possible contraction and extension of its own characteristics as an object made for movement.

Finally, we could say that whereas in a normal situation a car circulates into one direction, when the car looses this orbit it skids. After this skid the car can either come back to its earlier orbit or can stop (probably crash). But, what happens if this skidding becomes a continuum? then a new orbit is generated. The new ellipse after the abandonment, a new possible orbit of infinite screeching.

Ligne d'abandon was exhibited at the Chantal Crousel gallery in Paris, during Orozco's exhibition in December-January 1993-94.

Gabriel Orozco / Manuel Rocha, April 1996

A thing is a hole in a thing it is not.

Carl Andre

On making Something out of Nothing
Simon Glendinning

Martin Heidegger wanted to make something out of nothing. Infamously, he said such things as: '*Das Nichts selbst nichtet*' ('The Nothing itself nothings'). For many, this was quite enough to prove that Heidegger's work is dangerous nonsense, and there is no point reading it.

Remember the tiger who came to tea. He was very hungry. He ate all the sandwiches. All the buns on the dish. All the biscuits. All the cake. Until there was nothing left to eat on the table. And then he ate all the supper that was cooking in the saucepans and all the food in the fridge and all the packets and tins in the cupboard and all the orange juice and all Daddy's beer. And Mummy said, 'I don't know what to do. I've got nothing for supper.'[1]

And yet Heidegger would have us think that 'what is left' for supper here is still something 'positive'. Something 'insubstantial' no doubt, but it is whatever it is that is named by the 'nothing' in those sentences.

But Heidegger, Heidegger, it's a simple point. The word 'nothing' is not properly used as the name of something positive. And that is because it is not properly used as a name. Of course, the word 'nothing' does have a proper use. Like 'all', it is a quantifier. Quantifiers typically specify the extent of the range of things to which any predicate (F) may, in some Situation (S), truly be applied. So we have:

nothing is F in S = F has zero application in S

Not (as Heidegger must suppose):

nothing is F in S = there is some x which is F in S

The logician reminds us that 'nothing' is normally a quantifier. And quantifiers range over all the items in a given Situation. But now: what if Heidegger's use of 'nothing' is nothing other than a way of contrasting the being of a 'Situation' with the being of 'items' found within them? What if the being there of such a 'there' is the condition in which 'what is' (whatever quantifiers can range over) can be, say, 'visibly there'? And what if this 'there' is never an object that stands before us as something which might itself be seen there as an item among others? An 'ever-nonobjective' (as he also says) condition of every visibility, every predication or quantification. That is Heidegger's 'nothing'. Read on, it does no harm.

1. see *The Tiger Who Came to Tea* by Judith Kerr (first published by William Collins Sons & Co., London 1968)

opposite:
Postal Sculpture
Gilbert & George
1969

'ART FOR ALL' LONDON, 1969

*"All my life I give you nothing
and still you ask for more."*

from the sculptors

George. and Gilbert.

NO FUTURE

Maximum Penalty £5

Sex PiStols

Notes

FROM ZERO TO NOTHING IN NO TIME (pp.16–30)

1. 'The Problem of Meaning in Primitive Language', Bronislav Malinowski, in *The Meaning of Meaning: A Study of the Influence of Language Upon Thought and of The Science of Symbolism*, C K Ogden and I A Richards eds.; K Paul, Trench, Trubner & Co., London 1923

2. *Molloy*, Samuel Beckett, Knopf, New York 1955

3. 'There is no silence now', Jill Johnston, in *John Cage: An Anthology*, Richard Kostelanetz ed., Da Capo Press, New York 1991

4. *Silence*, John Cage, Marion Boyars, London 1999

5. *Miss Wyoming*, Douglas Coupland, Vintage, London 2000

6. 'Andy Warhol: Shadows', Lynne Cooke, *www.diacenter.org*, New York 1998

7. *Warhol*, Victor Bockris, Da Capo Press, New York 1997

8. *The Book of Revelation*, Rupert Thomson, Knopf, New York 1999

9. *The Book of Nothing*, John D Barrow, Pantheon Books, London 2000

10. *On Philosophy, Negotiations 1972–1990*, Columbia University Press 1991

11. *Slow Learner*, Thomas Pynchon, Little Brown, Mass. 1984

12. *Slow Learner*, *ibid.*

13. 'Sloth', Thomas Pynchon, in 'Nearer, my Couch, to Thee' in *The New York Times Book Review*, 6 June 1993

14. 'Big Game: Pynchon hunters find it frighteningly easy to track and catch their prey', David Bowman, *www.salon.com*, 22 September 1998

15. 'Lecture on Something', in *Silence, ibid.*

16. 'On Playing Feldman', John Tilbury, *www.cnvill.demon.co.uk/mftilb.htm*

17. 'Beckett as Librettist', Howard Skempton in *Music and Musicians*, May 1977

18. *Prisons of Light – Black Holes*, Kitty Ferguson, Cambridge University Press, 1998

19. from Holger Weh interview with Robert Barry, *www.mip.at/de/dokumente/1123-content.html*

20. 'Untitled', Robert Barry in *Theories and Documents of Contemporary Art: A Sourcebook of Artists' Writings*, Kristine Stiles and Peter Selz eds., University of California Press, 1996

21. Gerhard Richter in *The Daily Practice of Painting*, Gerhard Richter and Obrist eds., MIT Press, Boston, Mass. 1995

22. Gerhard Richter in *ibid.*

23. *Underworld*, Don DeLillo, Picador, London 1998

24. The Glass Bead Game, Hermann Hesse, Picador, London

25. *Warhol, ibid.*

26. *Logic of Events*, Charles S Pierce, 1898

27. *Warhol*, David Bourdon, Abrams, New York 1995

opposite:
No Future (sticker)
Jamie Reid
1976

FROM DAVID HUNTER TO ZERO
ALL IS GOD (essay pp.168–175)
1. from *Robert Smithson, The Collected Writings*, ed. Jack Flam, University of California Press, 1996
2. from *Islands of Truth – a Mathematical Mystery Cruise*, Ivars Peterson, W H Freeman & Co., 1990
3. from 'Solid Geometry' in *First Love, Last Rites*, Ian McEwan, Picador, London 1975

Sources (found and stolen):
phoenix.akasha.de/~aton/MerkImplant.html
www.maths.usyd.edu.au:8000/u/magma/htmlhelp/text549.html
www.bu.edu/wcp/Papers/Scie/ScieShpe.htm
www.wizvax.net/tap3x/EMGTI/j5hyperbody.html

opposite:
Untitled
Robert Barry
1969

Something which exists and of which I am aware, but I cannot know if anyone else is aware of it, or even can be aware of it.

Acknowledgements and Further Information

p.6 *I'm Completely Exhausted*
photo: Paul Ruscha

p.9 *Le saut dans le vide*
photo: Shunk-Kender; work (Leap into the Void): ©Yves Klein ADAGP, Paris and DACS, London 2001; photo: © Harry Shunk (The title of this work, following Klein's newspaper, '*Dimanche 27 novembre 1960*', is: '*Un homme dans l'espace! Le peintre l'espace se jette dans le vide!*', 1960)

p.14 floatation tank
courtesy of Floatworld Limited, *www.floatworld.com*

p.19 *Shadows*
photo (installation view): Jon Abbott, courtesy Dia Center for the Arts, New York; work: © The Andy Warhol Foundation for the Visual Arts, Inc./ARS, NY and DACS, London 2001

pp.25–26 excerpt from *The Life and Opinions of Tristram Shandy, Gentleman*
Volume 1, Chapter XII, Penguin, London 1997 (pp.29–30); suggested by Jonathan Watkins

p.31 still from *The Invisible Man*
sourced by Raimundas Malašauskas: 'I could only find one version of the film in Vilnius, which was made in the former USSR in 1984.'

pp.32–33 *Wiped Off The Face Of The Earth*
courtesy of the artist

p.34 *Condensation Cube*
photo: John Riddy, London; work: courtesy of the Lisson Gallery, London

p.35 *Der Wanderer über dem Nebelmeer* photo: © Elke Walford, Hamburg; work courtesy of Hamburger Kunsthalle

p.36 *Whirlpool (Eye of the Storm)*
created in El Mirage Dry Lake, Southern California: 3/4mile by 4-mile schemata of a vortex (whirlpool), traced in the sky using standard white smoke discharged by an aircraft

p.37 *Proposal for Vacuum*
photo: courtesy of the Armchair Mountaineering Club

p.38 *Artist in a Disappearing Landscape*
photo originally transmitted on-site, 10 December 1999 (via GSM): 'The thing that we are looking for is – by its very nature – absent from the present'

p.40 excerpt from *The Hunting of the Snark*
Penguin, London 1997 (p.56); suggested by David Ward

pp.42–43 *Chicago Board of Trade II*
courtesy of the artist, with thanks to Monika Sprüth Galerie, Köln

p.44 *Flextime/Coretime #7*
courtesy of private collection, London

p.45 Costa del Sol
photo: Graham Gussin

pp.46–47 *Observatory*
courtesy of the artist and the Government Art Collection

pp.48–53 *Report on an Unidentified Space Station*
story from the collection *War Fever*, published by Flamingo/HarperCollins, London, and Farrar, Straus & Giroux, New York; © J G Ballard, 1990; reproduced by permission of the author, c/o Margaret Hanbury, 27 Walcot Square, London SE11 4UB

p.54 image from CERN particle accelerator
collection of Keith Wilson

p.56 *Map of a thirty-six square mile surface area of the Pacific Ocean west of Oahu*
courtesy of the artists and Lisson Gallery, London

p.57 *Untitled, 1969*
© ARS, NY and DACS, London 2001; with thanks to Leo Castelli Gallery, New York

p.58 Anechoic chamber
photo: Graham Gussin

pp.62–63 *Steam (second version)*
© ARS, NY and DACS, London 2001; courtesy of Leo Castelli Gallery, New York

pp.64–76 'Is It Out There?'
Chapter 12 from *The Nothing That Is*, published by Allen Lane The Penguin Press, London 1999; © Robert Kaplan, 1999; reproduced by permission of the author, and The Penguin Press, London, and Oxford University Press Inc., New York

pp.70–71 *Add & Subtract*
Dolores Zinny and Juan Maidagan

p.77 *Big Nothing*
pencil and eraser on paper, 250 x 150cm; courtesy the artist

pp.78–82 *The Book of Sand*
story from the collection *The Book of Sand*, published by Penguin Books, 1979; translation taken from *Collected Fictions*, translated by Andrew Hurley, © 1998 by Maria Kodama, translation © 1998 by Penguin Putnam., Inc.; reproduced by permission of Viking Penguin, a division of Penguin Putnam Inc., New York

p.83 *The Long Winter of Mars*
courtesy of the artist

pp.84–88 excerpt from *Book of Dust – The Beginning and the End of Time and Thereafter*
published by Visual Studies Workshop, Rochester, New York 1989; © Agnes Denes; reproduced by permission of the author

p.89 *Gap Fillers*
found object, mixed media; with thanks to Jeanette Holden

pp.90–91 excerpt from 'Lecture on Nothing'
in *Silence – Lectures and Writings*, published by Marion Boyars, London 1999; reproduced by permission of the publisher

pp.92–93 margin notes on *Creative Evolution*
Creative Evolution by Henri Bergson, published by University Press of America, Lanham MD 1983 (first published 1911)

pp.94–95 *A Place Where Nothing Has Happened*
courtesy of the artist

pp.98–99 death row merchandise
suggested by Adam Chodzko

p.100 *Untitled (police report of stolen invisible artwork)*
courtesy of the artist; thanks to Marian Goodman Gallery, New York

pp.101–106 *On Invisibility in Art*
with thanks to *Frieze*

p.107 *Understudy A*
courtesy of the artist

pp.108–109 *Untitled*
re-set from a work typewritten on paper; courtesy of the artist; thanks to Galerie Bugdahn und Kaimer, Düsseldorf

pp.112–113 *Untitled*
courtesy of the artist (from the series *Material*)

p.114 *Untitled*
courtesy of the artist (from the series *Material*)

p.115 cover of *Solaris*
Science Fiction Book Club, Newton Abbot, 1973

pp.116–117 *Intensities and Surfaces*
Wapping Pumping Station, London: 34 tonnes ice (3 x 3 x 4m) with a 1/2-tonne boulder of rock salt – melt period 3 months; courtesy of the artist

p.118 still from *Conical Intersect*
© ARS, NY and DACS, London 2001; courtesy of David Zwirner Gallery, New York

p.119 *Nothing 1*
oil on canvas, 200 x 180cm; courtesy of Anthony Wilkinson Gallery, London

p.122 *Garbage Bag*
photo: Andrew Whittuck, London; work courtesy of Lisson Gallery, London

p.123 *LAP Project*
taken on the A12, this image forms part of a series of photographs of 9 different disused petrol stations, all shot on 18 May 1998. The LAP project hoped to situate a drive-by/drive-through installation in an empty petrol station; it still remains virtual

p.124 *Black Bunting*
courtesy of the artist

p.125 *Closed*
neon sign, 40 x 12cm; courtesy the artist

p.126 *Puddle*
photo: Peter White; courtesy Kenny Schachter and Illona Rich

p.127 documentary photo of *Time Landscape*
photo: © Natural Cultural Landscapes™

p.129 *Drain*
photo: Geoffrey Clements; courtesy of the artist

p.130 still from *The Dilapidated Dwelling*
duration: 78 mins, Beta SX; still shows methane burner at capped landfill in former chalk quarry (site of planned station for Channel Tunnel rail link), near Northfleet, Kent

p.131 still from *Film of me hiding in the bushes*
16mm colour film, duration 6 minutes

p.132 production shot of *220V, 2.2kW*
fuel, generator, lights, sound (duration: 5 minutes, 30 seconds); courtesy the artist; special thanks to Joehari Lee and Philipos Kapa

p.133 *Strollogy, Cloud Walk 7*
work comprises: walking stick, oak box (partially lined with blue velvet), sealed 2000ml separating funnel (containing cloud), Pathfinder(1:25000), document

with data and descriptions, documentary photographs; courtesy of the artist

pp.134–135 *Sometimes nothing leads to something*
courtesy of the artist

pp.136–137 *Sometimes something leads to nothing*
courtesy of the artist

p.138 *Untitled*
'On 5 March 1969, somewhere in the Mojave Desert, 2 cubic feet of helium was returned to the atmosphere'; courtesy of the artist

p.142 *Wested Interchange (detail 4)*
courtesy Emily Tsingou Gallery, London

p.143 excerpt from *Roadside Picnic* published by Macmillan, London 1977 (pp.7–9); reproduced by permission of Victor Gollancz, London and Franz Rottensteiner, Vienna

pp.143–158 by Gaia Alessi
1. phantasm. a figment of the imagination; an illusion or apparition. – ORIGIN via Latin from Greek *phantasma*, from *phantazeine* 'make visible'; from *phaineine* 'to show'
2. see *The Logic of Sense* by Gilles Deleuze, The Athlone Press, London 1990 (pp.210-216)

p.144 excerpt from *The Aesthetics of Disappearance*
published by Semiotext(e), New York 1991 (pp.9-11); reproduced by permission of Autonomedia, New York

p.162 Black Hole
photo: Robert Nemiroff, sourced from *www.antwrp.gsfc.nasa.gov*

pp.163–165 Black Holes
essay from *The Faber Book of Science*, John Carey, ed., Faber & Faber, London 1995 (reproduced from *The Roving Mind: A Panoramic View of Fringe Science, Technology, and the Mind of the Future*, Prometheus Books, 1983); reproduced by permission of the Estate of Isaac Asimov c/o Ralph M Vicinanza, Ltd. (New York)

p.166 David Cunningham

p.167 Janka Vukmir (on the work of Slaven Tolj), Zagreb 1995

pp.170–171 excerpt from 'Solid Geometry'
taken from *First Love, Last Rites*, published by Jonathan Cape; reproduced by permission of The Random House Group Limited.

p.172 *Spiral Jetty*
photo: Gianfranco Gorgoni, courtesy James Cohan Gallery, New York; collection: DIA Center for the Arts, New York; © Estate of Robert Smithson/VAGA, New York/DACS, London 2001

p.179 *3 No-Plays*
with thanks to Jon Hendricks of The Gilbert and Lila Silverman Collection, New York

p.183 *Total Eclipse*
newspaper collage; courtesy of Lisson Gallery, London

pp.184–187 *How the World Was Saved*
story from *The Cyberiad: Fables for the Cybernetic Age*, published by Harvest, 1985; English translation by Michael Kandel © 1974 by Harcourt, Inc., Florida; reprinted by permission of the publisher

p.189 article
© *The Guardian*, 11 August 2000 (Tim Radford)

pp.190–191 *Some Void Thoughts on Museums*
image (*The Museum of the Void*):

pp.192–193 from sleeve for *Ligne d'abandon*
courtesy of the artists, with thanks to Chantal Crousel Gallery, Paris

p.197 *Postal Sculpture 1969*
courtesy of Andrew Wilson (postcard sent to the fellow participants in the *18 Paris IV, 70* exhibition)

p.198 *No Future sticker*
courtesy of Stolper-Wilson Collection, London

p.201 *Untitled*
re-set from a work typewritten on paper; courtesy of the artist; thanks to Galerie Bugdahn und Kaimer, Düsseldorf